THE BULLY ACTION GUIDE

HOW TO HELP YOUR CHILD AND GET YOUR SCHOOL TO LISTEN

EDWARD F. DRAGAN, EdD

D0168049

palgrave
macmillan

Names have been changed in some instances to protect the privacy of individuals. However, where individuals hold public office or in situations where names have been revealed through the media, the true names are used.

THE BULLY ACTION GUIDE
Copyright © Edward F. Dragan, 2011.

First published in 2011 by PALGRAVE MACMILLAN® in the U.S.—a division of St. Martin's Press LLC, 175 Fifth Avenue, New York, NY 10010.

Where this book is distributed in the UK, Europe and the rest of the world, this is by Palgrave Macmillan, a division of Macmillan Publishers Limited, registered in England, company number 785998, of Houndmills, Basingstoke, Hampshire RG21 6XS.

Palgrave Macmillan is the global academic imprint of the above companies and has companies and representatives throughout the world.

Palgrave® and Macmillan® are registered trademarks in the United States, the United Kingdom, Europe and other countries.

ISBN: 978-0-230-11042-7

Library of Congress Cataloging-in-Publication Data
Dragan, Edward F.
   The bully action guide : how to help your child and get your school to listen / Edward F. Dragan.
      p. cm.
   Includes index.
   ISBN 978-0-230-11042-7
   1. Bullying in schools—Prevention.   2. Bullying—Prevention.
3. Parenting.   I. Title.
LB3013.3.D73   2010
371.5'8—dc22

                                                                    2010042844

A catalogue record of the book is available from the British Library.

Design by Letra Libre, Inc.

First edition: May 2011

10 9 8 7 6 5 4 3 2 1

Printed in the United States of America.

PRAISE FOR *THE BULLY ACTION GUIDE*

"This book is an indispensable tool and support for parents of children dealing with bullying issues in school. Ed Dragan empowers parents to take action and protect their children from harassment and teaches them to intervene effectively with teachers and principals."

—Jodee Blanco, *New York Times* bestselling
author of *Please Stop Laughing at Me*

"In my work I see many understandably frustrated parents become desperate to figure out how to enlist the school when their child is bullied. How should they approach the teacher? What happens if the teacher won't recognize the problem? What should you do if the school refuses to do anything to stop the bullies? *The Bully Action Guide* fills a critical gap in the resources available for parents. Not only does it provide clear strategies for when to approach educators but how. The book is filled with simple yet powerful scripts for parents to use to clearly communicate their child's rights and hold educators responsible in a way that gives the parent the best chance of working in collaboration with the school. I am strongly recommending this book for all parents."

—Rosalind Wiseman, author of *Queen Bees and Wannabes*

"*The Bully Action Guide* is a must-have for anyone who is concerned about a child being bullied. Offering calm but effective dialogue templates, a 'chain of command' hierarchy to follow when results aren't forthcoming at one level, and tips on what to document and how, Dr. Dragan provides the steps to help both parents and authorities communicate more effectively."

—Cheryl Dellasega, author of *Mean Girls Grown Up*

"*The Bully Action Guide* is a priceless resource for any parent, grandparent and family member wanting to ensure their child's safety."

—Maureen Healy, author of
365 Perfect Things to Say to Your Kids

"A most important book for any parent whose child is being bullied! No other book gives parents such sensible, easy-to-follow guidance for helping a child who's being bullied and effectively communicating with a school to end the bullying. A must-read."

—Naomi Drew, author of *No Kidding about Bullying*

"Bullying is not a rite of passage; it is abuse that must be stopped. Dragan skillfully provides 'how to's' that parents can follow to protect their children at school. Who to call, what to say, questions to ask, and scripts to follow—words so potent that they cannot be ignored. You want this pro on your team in times of trouble. He is telling you exactly how schools operate and how to get what you need. Listen and be safe!"

—Mary Jo McGrath, author of *School Bullying:*
Tools for Avoiding Harm and Liability

"Dragan's book places into the hands of parents orderly, commonsense procedures to effectively communicate with their child and with the school to end bullying. It is time for a step-by-step proven system to give parents the edge when dealing with school administrators and teachers. This book gives parents much needed tools, so that schools will not only listen to them but act to stop the bullying for their child."

—Brenda High, codirector and founder of
watchdog organization Bully Police USA

"*The Bully Action Guide* makes it easy for parents to understand their rights and how to get help for their bullied child. This bullying risk-management guide should be mandatory reading for parents and especially for school administrators."

—Parry Aftab, executive director of WiredSafety
and author of *The Parent's Guide to Protecting*
Your Children in Cyberspace

This book is dedicated to all parents who care about their children. It is my hope that this book will empower parents with the knowledge and skills to intervene with schools to save their children from the harms of bullying.

Also, this book is dedicated to Dolores, my wonderful wife, and our terrific grandchildren—Silas, Victoria, Leon, Kayla, Sophia, Joseph, and Noelle.

CONTENTS

ACKNOWLEDGMENTS

I would like to acknowledge Michael Dalzell for his assistance with manuscript preparation; my agent, Jessica Papin, of Dystel and Goderich Literary Management, and Luba Ostashevsky, editor at Palgrave Macmillan, for believing that what I have to say is important and would give parents the information they need to help their children; and a special thanks to Sadika Jubo, my assistant, who put up with the deadlines not only for the book but for reports on our cases and kept me on track.

INTRODUCTION

I have spent 40 years in education. At various times in my career, I was a special-education teacher, founded an alternative school with a group of disenchanted students and parents, worked as an administrator and teacher in a residential treatment center for disturbed children, served as a public school principal and superintendent, and was an education manager for the New Jersey Department of Education. I am now a litigation consultant and expert witness in education. I have pretty much seen it all in schools. I've witnessed kids teasing, taunting, and beating each other up for lots of different reasons.

As a new teacher in the late 1960s, I assumed that teachers and administrators had the best interests of students in mind and that children would treat each other nicely. I was 22 years old, just married, and trying to figure out how not to be drafted into the Vietnam War. Special-education teachers were in short supply at that time. And the job came with a deferment, so I took it.

I walked into a classroom where the only course materials were discarded library books and where the kids, ranging from 7 to 15 years of age, were at each other's throats. Many of the older kids couldn't read. In this environment, my first challenge was to help the students treat each other with more respect. My next task was to create a climate in the larger school community where the other kids didn't make fun of the students in my class because they walked funny or didn't communicate clearly. For schools, these are universal challenges.

In college, I read *Lord of the Flies,* which had a profound impact on my philosophy of education. In it, a group of stranded children develop their own culture in which the most ruthless kids dominate. With no adult moral compass, animal instincts rule until the group commits the ultimate act of bullying—killing the child whom they identify as the "pig." In my first class, I quickly learned the importance of prompt, firm adult intervention when kids treat other kids badly. I had to create a culture that helped children learn to be good people as well as good students.

Later, when my wife, Dolores, and I adopted two girls and a boy—all dark skinned—we learned much more about bullying as we suffered with them through racial harassment. One of our daughters was also learning disabled and was tormented for that. As teachers, it was easy for Dolores and me to see how children behaved toward one another in class. As parents, it was harder to find out what was going on with our own children.

How do you know that your own child is being harassed? Signs may be as obvious as bruises or as subtle as behavior changes or falling grades. You may barely notice something wrong with your child or perceive his problems as inconsequential. With the information in this book—drawn from my experience and the ordeals of people whom I have helped—you can learn to spot bullying, talk with your children about it, and stop it from escalating.

You will learn how to defuse a bullying situation by communicating effectively with the school. There are many stages of interaction with schools, and each requires a unique reaction to get school officials to listen. As an insider who knows how schools work, I will give you a step-by-step guide that teaches you the following:

- whom to call at the school
- what to say and what to ask the school to do
- what questions to ask to get the facts about bullying in your child's school
- what to write in a letter to get the school to act
- when to move up the chain of command if you get no satisfaction

I consult with parents whose children have been killed, injured, humiliated, or bullied in school, usually after it is too late and they have sued the district. *The Bully Action Guide* is dedicated to those children, in the hope that the information I provide will help you before matters get that far. Information confers power. With power comes change: a better education and a more hopeful life for your child.

REAL-LIFE STORIES

With authority and empathy, *The Bully Action Guide* taps into an urgent, ongoing national conversation among parents.

This book tells the stories of real people. Why? There are already plenty of books that give you a menu of options, but stories tell the harassment experience through the eyes of the victim—the most compelling way to help you understand what you should or should not do. After all, your journey into understanding the world of school-based harassment begins with a story—your child's story.

A child who came to be one of my own clients, seventh-grader Patrick Ferry,[1] found himself on TV talk shows after posting a gripping video on YouTube chronicling his own yearlong bullying experience. His horror ended only when his mother called the police after a bully tried to smash his head with a rock. Patrick's seven-minute documentary was a cry for help after school authorities repeatedly refused to intervene. Within days of its appearance online, the video had been seen by tens of thousands of young people— many of whom went on to post their own heart-rending stories of bullying agony.

For her part, Patrick's mother didn't know how to deal with his hurt or how to get the school to listen. Beth Ferry didn't know that she should have called the school, followed up with a letter, and held the school accountable. Doing this would have placed the school on notice that she was a parent with knowledge—one not to be shuffled aside and told, "Don't worry—we'll take care of it." If Beth had this book, she would have known how to protect Patrick by holding the school to that promise.

The stories in this book, like that of Patrick, are true accounts of bullying that no parent would want to experience. Almost always, these ordeals can be averted by strategic use of parental radar—asking the right questions and stepping in decisively at key moments. Education experts have learned a lot about what works in this area and what doesn't. And from that, I have made a system—one that you can learn to help you break through often well-meaning, but ineffective, school bureaucracy; be heard; and get results.

SCHOOLS DON'T GET IT

After the Columbine massacre—which was allegedly sparked in part by the merciless treatment endured by Eric Harris and Dylan Klebold, the two teenage mass murderers—there was a great deal of talk about eliminating bullying in schools. And how did that turn out?

In Columbine's aftermath, many school districts ultimately did nothing—or nothing new. Others tried a patchwork of antibullying programs, most of them unproven and usually resulting in no significant impact on student behavior. Many schools adopted a "zero tolerance" standard, as though bullying could be stamped out entirely. Police were stationed in schools, and children were handcuffed and arrested for making meaningless schoolyard comments or for unsubstantiated rumors of threats. Other than needlessly traumatizing young people, zero tolerance has had zero effect on the problem, because punishment alone is no solution. A school culture long inured to bullying isn't changed by locking up bullies.

As parents, we need to know that many methods that schools use to deal with bullying are counterproductive. For instance, forcing a bully to apologize to a victim usually guarantees that the victim will get beaten up again for his trouble. Or school officials may tell you to dismiss a persistent rumor about how your child is being treated at school as not worthy of your attention. Such rumors, however, are usually true—if the grapevine says the skater kids are picking on your child, it's best to believe it.

As much as we would like to believe that schools are protecting our children, the sad truth is that school systems have little incentive to reach out to parents when their children are being bullied. School administrators like to keep everything operating smoothly. No noise from parents keeps the lid on. This book will show you how to step in, open the lid, and compel the school to act.

You will learn how to cut through red tape, resistance, and poor follow-through. I will teach you how to take charge when the school shows little or no interest. Unlike any other, this book provides sample scripts for telephone conversations with school officials and sample letters to send to administrators. It takes you behind the door of the principal's office and explains (from the point of view of someone who has been there) how the system works—and how to make it work for you.

An episode of bullying is a teachable moment. To teach is to change. Use this book to teach, to change the climate in your child's school, and to institute a positive culture.

THREE MESSAGES, ONE SIMPLE METHOD

My antibullying system for parents is based on three messages:

1. *All abusive behavior is bullying.* In the overwhelming majority of cases, bullying will not go away of its own accord.
2. *Bullying is an outrage.* Society should not stand for it—ever.
3. *You can do something about it.* When parents learn how to communicate effectively with the school, they can turn this outrage into a teachable moment. More accurately, bullying is a *teachable outrage* on which we can capitalize to change schools for the better.

Learning to manage the school environment is vital not only when it comes to bullying, but also when it comes to the equally pernicious problem of difference-based discrimination. This includes harassment based on ethnicity, race, religion, and—more and more frequently—gender identity, as children begin to identify themselves as gay or bisexual at earlier ages. *The Bully Action Guide* provides a single harassment concept that will give you answers for all these situations. No other book does this.

How hard you want to push depends on you and what needs to be accomplished. When it comes to protecting a child, public schools offer many more levers to pull than private schools. In public schools, there is a hierarchy that is wired to respond to parental pressure—from principal to superintendent and up through the state and federal bureaucracies—every member of which serves at taxpayer expense. Moving your child to a private school in the hope that this will stave off bullying is usually misguided. We may think that in exchange for paying a hefty tab, private institutions offer a refuge from the harsher world of public education, or—at the very least—that the headmaster will take our complaints seriously. Precisely the opposite is often true: parents usually have *less* control at a private institution. With that in mind, I will give you effective, simple strategies for dealing with top administrators at both public and private schools.

UNDERSTANDING YOUR CHILD'S HURTS

Harassment and bullying cut a wide path: hurtful comments, physical aggression, social isolation, and destruction of property. The latest incarnation, cyberbullying, is perverse and cruel because aggressors can hide beneath a cloak of anonymity and spread their venom rapidly. For all the attention that cyberbullying has received, however, most bullying still occurs face-to-face, in places children spend most of their time interacting with society: at school, on the school bus, and at school-sponsored events.

Regardless of the form it takes, bullying has two key components: repeated harmful acts and an imbalance of power. Not all taunting, teasing, and fighting among school children constitute bullying. When acts are repeated by someone perceived as physically or psychologically more powerful—that is bullying.

Most students do not report bullying to adults at school or at home. Because of this, schools underestimate the extent of the problem, and parents don't always know that their children are victims. Kids think they won't be believed, they don't want to worry their parents, or they don't think anything would change if they told someone. The kids are right. Many school administrators trivialize bullying because the people involved are children. That should not happen. Bullying is a potentially life-altering event.

So what do you do when you suspect your child is being bullied at school?

It's not easy to get information from kids—especially if they are afraid or embarrassed about the situation. You can overcome this by creating an atmosphere of trust. When your child comes to you and says, "Jason called me a retard," or "Patty keeps tripping me on the playground," listen more than talk. Ask questions without being judgmental. In this book, you'll learn skills for getting your child to open up to you—a critical first step toward leveraging the teachable outrage in your child's school.

IT COULD SAVE A CHILD'S LIFE

If Phoebe Prince's mother had this book, she would have known that just telling the principal that her daughter was bullied at her prior school was not enough. Phoebe was bullied in Ireland—one of the reasons she and her mother, Anne O'Brien, moved to Massachusetts. When Phoebe's mother told administrators at her daughter's new school, South Hadley High School, about this, they reassured her not to worry—telling her that they would watch out for Phoebe and that Phoebe would be safe.

Ms. O'Brien did not document that discussion with a follow-up letter. She did not ask for a copy of South Hadley's antiharassment policy. She did not ask administrators for a plan of intervention if Phoebe were to be bullied in their school. She did not establish a liaison with a staff member who could check on Phoebe periodically and report to Ms. O'Brien. She didn't fail to do these things because she was a bad mother who was indifferent to her child's sufferings; rather, she didn't do these things because she did not know she should have.

Phoebe told her mother that the "mean girls" were picking on her at her new school—even calling her a whore in the cafeteria and the library and loudly berating her in class in front of a teacher. Like many parents, Ms. O'Brien trusted the school to do the right thing and to protect her daughter. If Ms. O'Brien had had this book, she would have known to call the school and document that she notified South Hadley about Phoebe's vulnerability. She would have had a script for that telephone call and a sample letter to force the school to follow up on its obligation to protect Phoebe from the harms of bullying. If Ms. O'Brien would have known that she had the ability to foment decisive action, Phoebe might not have taken her own life.

All over America, the same story plays out day in, day out. Parents suspect something is not right with their child, but they trust the school to handle it or are made to feel neurotic or overprotective when they voice their concerns.

This book is for you—the parent who finds himself or herself in the same situation. The ideas presented in this book are drawn from my own experiences in real schools—public and private; rural, suburban, and urban; rich and poor—through my work as a litigation consultant to hundreds of attorneys who represent bullied students or defend schools accused of negligence when students were bullied. These methods get results. I have taught these steps to anxiety-ridden parents who were lost for what to do. I have seen dozens of children saved from the harms of bullying when their parents followed the steps in this book.

A HOW-TO MANUAL

The Bully Action Guide is about taking action—it's about how you can stop the outrage of bullying by effectively interacting with your child's school. As more and more high-profile bullying cases push this outrage over new legal thresholds, it's in a school's best interest to deal with an informed parent—instead of a lawyer.

The proven steps in this book are crafted through my twin perspectives: that of a father and grandfather of children who have been harassed and that of an insider who knows the system. I know what works, what doesn't, and how parents can tell the difference. If parents had this book when I was a school administrator, I surely would have acted decisively if they had called armed with this knowledge.

The Bully Action Guide is an authoritative parenting book that will give you confidence and empowerment in a school environment where you may find few sympathetic ears.

CHAPTER ONE

THE MANY FACES OF BULLYING

KEYCEPT: School should be a place where children feel safe and secure—a place where they can count on being treated with respect. The unfortunate reality is that many students are the targets of bullying, resulting in long-term academic, physical, and emotional consequences. School personnel often minimize or underestimate the extent of bullying and its harm. In many cases, bullying is tolerated or ignored.

The school bully has been around forever. The stereotypical bully—the schoolyard tough guy who is quick to fight, intimidate, and threaten for his own gain or to look good in front of other kids—has become so much a part of the school environment that, in some situations, school administrators consider this intrusion into the school culture as the norm. This response is unfortunate in light of today's understanding about the scope of bullying and the psychological damage it inflicts—up to the point of suicide.

Today's bully isn't just the schoolyard punk who shoves other kids around or double-dog dares them. It's the seventh-grade girl who tells lies about a classmate to keep her out of the "girl group."

It's the handsome student council president who pushes a wheel-chair-bound child into a wall. It's the tenth grader who says something on Facebook about someone that she wouldn't have the guts to say to her face. It's the aide on a school bus who sexually assaults a four-year-old while sitting next to him. It's the teacher whose punishment of a student doesn't fit the "crime." Bullies can be athletic, academically smart, attractive, and cunning. School administrators don't see them in the crowd. They blend in and work under the radar. They bully when no one is looking and intimidate their victims, who are too afraid to tell.

Today, it's more urgent than ever that parents learn new techniques for dealing with these situations.

EXTENT OF BULLYING

Let's first take a look at what's happening in our nation's schools.

Various reports have established that 15 percent of students are either bullied or are initiators of bullying behavior on a regular basis.[1] Almost 30 percent of sixth- through tenth-grade youths in the United States (more than 5.7 million kids) are thought to be involved in bullying as either a bully, a target of bullying, or both.[2] In a 2001 national survey of students, 13 percent reported bullying others, 11 percent reported being the target of bullies, and another 6 percent said that they both bullied others and were bullied themselves.[3]

A large survey of sixth- through tenth-grade students by the National Institute of Child Health and Human Development reveals the breadth of the problem:[4]

- 37 percent have been victims of verbal harassment.
- 32 percent have been subjected to rumor spreading.
- 26 percent have experienced social isolation.

- 13 percent have been assaulted physically.
- 10 percent have been cyberbullied.

The relationship between "traditional" (or direct, face-to-face) bullying and cyberbullying is interesting; more than 6 of every 10 cybervictims have been subjected to traditional bullying.[5] Because most children who are bullied directly are tortured at the hands of classmates, it should come as no surprise that there is frequently a school component to cyberbullying.

Face-to-face bullying increases through the elementary years, peaks in the middle school / junior high school years, and declines during the high school years. While physical assault decreases with age, however, verbal abuse remains constant. A school's size, racial composition, and setting (rural, suburban, or urban) are not distinguishing factors in predicting the occurrence of bullying. Boys, however, engage in, and are victims of, bullying behavior more frequently than girls.[6]

When teachers and administrators fail to intervene, some victims ultimately take things into their own hands—often with grievous results. In a recent analysis of 37 school shooting incidents, the U.S. Secret Service reported that a majority of shooters had suffered "bullying and harassment that was longstanding and severe."[7] In many other cases, bullying has prompted suicides among our children. The use of the Internet only worsens the cycle of ugliness, with suicide victims being maligned online after their deaths and anonymous websites subsequently springing up, dedicated to berating those who still bully even after their victim's death.

Though bullying is a fact of life, it clearly has negative repercussions on children, and parents want to know what they can do to stop it. And sometimes, this requires parental intervention. That's what this book is about—how you, as a caring parent, can do something about bullying. This book is for the mother who needs to intervene when she finds out that her daughter is being excluded from the girl group that spreads rumors about her. It's for the father who needs to intervene when he finds out that his son was called a fag on the playground and had been tripped by an older student. It's for the parents who have been stonewalled by school administrators and who need to make the school live up to its duty to protect their child.

Almost 30 percent of kids in the United States are thought to be involved in bullying as either a bully, a target of bullying, or both.

WHAT IS BULLYING?

Bullying can be a severe single occurrence intended to hurt someone physically or emotionally. More often, a key component of bullying is a series of events that, over time, creates an ongoing pattern of harassment.[8] Either way, it always includes an unequal distribution of power between two people or groups of people. Two boys of the same age and size getting into a fight is not bullying, but a child who hurts another child in a situation where one has power and the other does not is bullying. The power dynamic may be size or age, but it also could be class, race, sexuality, gender, a disability, or something else. The success of the bully is predicated on arrogant disregard for simple decency and a willingness to brutalize an innocent, vulnerable person simply because the bully is stronger and others are unwilling to intervene.

My granddaughter is a 14-year-old child with Down syndrome. One day, on the way to the bus, the teacher felt that Victoria was not listening and took her to a "time-out" room. During a call to

Victoria's mother, the teacher said, "If she doesn't listen, you'll have to pick her up from school. She won't be allowed to take the bus. By the way, when she was in the isolation room she took off all her clothes and was screaming and banging on the wall." Victoria isn't able to speak clearly because of an expressive language disorder. She wasn't able to tell her mom that the teacher had put her in a six-by-six-foot cinder-block room at least four times recently for "fooling around." Victoria's inability to communicate clearly frustrated the teacher and led her to bully Victoria.

In another story of teacher bullying, a North Carolina middle school teacher wrote the word *LOSER* on his student's paper. Other students saw the paper and felt emboldened to turn against their classmate. Luckily, the student's mother also saw the paper—her son hadn't volunteered the information to her—and she contacted the principal. The teacher was suspended for two weeks without pay and was mandated to undergo professional and ethical training before returning to the classroom. The superintendent also required the teacher to write a letter of apology to the student. In his own defense, the teacher said he was trying to relate to students by using their lingo, but the school's administration made it clear in a statement that the teacher's action was irresponsible: "Regardless of the intention or context, demeaning or derogatory comments made to students by school staff are unacceptable and will not be rationalized or justified by the school system."[9]

Contrast the North Carolina superintendent's swift and appropriate action with that of the principal at Brooklyn's PS 161, where kindergarten bullies punched five-year-old Jazmin and cut off her hair. Somehow, the students were allowed access to scissors. One has to question the supervision in this class. Jazmin's mom and grandmother said Jazmin endured months of anguish during a year in which most children enjoy story time and snacks. "This is too much for her," said

Jazmin's grandmother. "She's waking up screaming in the middle of the night, saying someone's hitting her." Jazmin was hit in the face, and her lunch was knocked to the floor. Later, she was beaten in the bathroom and came home missing a big clump of hair, telling her mother that another child had lopped off her braids. "When I saw that bald spot in the back of her head, I was about to cry," said Yvonne, her mother. "I'm scared to have her go to school." And so is Jazmin, who once couldn't wait to walk to school in the morning but now has to be dragged, literally, to it. Still, the principal denied there was a problem: "I know that Jazmin isn't mistreated in the classroom. We have all the other kindergartners in the school, and they're fine."[10]

It's not uncommon for administrators to take the stance, "If I say it didn't happen or it can't happen in my school, I don't have to deal with it and this parent." We'll talk more about this in chapter two.

And what about my personal experience with bullying?

I got my share as a child. While in the sixth grade at St. Joseph's Elementary School, I had a run-in with the boys in my class. I don't know where they got the rope, but at least three kids pushed me down, held me on the ground, and tied my feet and hands. The bell rang, I struggled, and they ran. The shame and humiliation I experienced was extreme. And to this day, I sometimes think of that pain. Somehow, I wriggled from the restraints and sadly made my way up to the door of the principal's office for a late pass. I would never tell what happened. I was too humiliated.

"Why are you late?" I was asked.

"Oh, I didn't hear the bell 'cause I was over by the ball field."

Quite a lie to tell a nun—who also happened to be the principal! A double lie, so I thought. But like many kids, I felt justified in keeping the secret. Why didn't I stand up to these three older and stronger boys? Because I thought I was a weakling and I didn't want anyone—the nun, my parents, or anyone else—to know that. Not only that, but those kids had smirked at me as if to say, "Mess with us, and we'll do it again."

A key component of bullying is a series of events that, over time, creates an ongoing pattern of harassment.

TYPES OF BULLYING

Whether perpetrated by kids, teachers, or others, bullying takes on many forms: sexual, disability, and gender-identity harassment; ethnic, religious, and racial harassment; lies and innuendo; hazing or initiation into a group; and harassing phone and text messages, to name several. Generally, there are four broad types of bullying: physical, verbal, social, and cyber.

Physical bullying may include hitting, kicking, pushing, or spitting on another child. It can also include damage to property or theft of property. When most people think of bullying, this is what they imagine.

Verbal bullying, which may be used along with other forms of bullying, includes name-calling, teasing, threats, and misuse of authority. Racial, sexual, and homophobic epithets are considered verbal bullying.

Social bullying relies on groups and relationships within those groups. Forms of social bullying include spreading rumors, exclusion from a group, and positioning someone to take the blame for something they did not do.

Cyberbullying, also known as electronic bullying, is done via the Internet or through the use of cell phones. This type of bullying occurs through texting, email, online games, instant messaging, videos or photographs, and chat rooms. Cyberbullying can include sending threatening or vulgar messages or images, posting private information about someone online, or posing as someone else in an attempt to make the intended victim look bad.

Boys and girls bully differently. Boys tend to use physical aggression. Bullying is also more socially acceptable among boys and the adults who supervise them. Bullying in the macho world of sports is still reinforced; even after so many lawsuits directed at coaches who have allowed bullying or hazing—and in some cases, even encouraged it—it still takes place. What do we teach our kids when a coach laughs at a group of boys who taunt the weaker one who can't run as fast as the others?

Girls who bully are more apt to engage in more indirect forms of aggression, such as social isolation.[11] Girls tend to bully other girls by gossiping about them. Girls are also more likely to be the target of sexual bullying, which may include rumors about their sexual activities.[12] Because girls' bullying behavior is often more covert, schools and parents may not notice it quickly.

Though bullying comes in many stripes, each form of bullying should be fought in the same way—a way that will allow you to learn how to penetrate the schoolhouse, open the door to the principal's office, and become an active participant in the protection of your child. This book will teach you how to recognize bullying and nip it in the bud before it takes on a life of its own.

WHY ARE SOME KIDS BULLIES?

There are three interrelated reasons why students bully:

1. *Bullies have a strong need for power and control.* Bullying is purely about power and about capitalizing on an imbalance of it by intimidating a weaker, more vulnerable child.

2. *Bullies find satisfaction in causing injury or suffering to other students.* They share a lack of empathy for others and may have positive attitudes about violence.

3. *Bullies are often rewarded in some way, materially or psychologically, for their behavior.* Psychologically, the reasons are complex, but one factor that contributes to bullying is having parents who rarely show warmth, leading the child to seek appreciation from peers.

In fact, parenting and family relations play a large part in the emergence of a bully persona. Some bullies have parents who are overly permissive, set few limits, or do not supervise their children well. Bullies also frequently have other "bully role models," such as their own parents, older siblings, or friends who bully and harbor an acceptance of violence.

You might not be surprised to learn that bullying in childhood is a gateway to significant behavior problems in adulthood. Studies in Scandinavian countries have established a strong correlation between bullying during the school years and experiencing legal troubles during the adult years. In one study, 60 percent of those characterized as bullies in grades six to nine had at least one criminal conviction by age 24.[13] Chronic bullies maintain their behaviors into adulthood and have difficulty with positive relationships.[14] All of these facts are good reasons to seize bullying as a teachable moment and intervene—not just for the sake of the victim, but for that of the bully, too.

WHY ARE SOME KIDS BULLIED?

If you are reading this book, chances are your child is being bullied or has experienced bullying at some point in time. Why?

Sometimes, there is little rhyme or reason for it—the bully simply thrives on what he perceives as superiority over your child. There are, however, several factors that make some kids more likely to be bullied than others.

Some children may unintentionally exhibit certain behaviors that can make them a target. Do any of these apply to your child?

- does not make good eye contact
- is upset easily by (or does not understand) teasing and reacts strongly to it
- does not understand body language or other nonverbal cues
- tends to misinterpret some benign words or actions as aggressive and reacts fearfully

When children who exhibit these behaviors are taught appropriate interpersonal skills, their chances of being snubbed by their peers are reduced.

Children who are typically anxious, insecure, or who suffer from low self-esteem rarely defend themselves or retaliate when confronted by students who bully them.[15] These children are often socially isolated and lack social skills.[16] In one study, children said that the main reason they thought kids were bullied was because the victims just "didn't fit in."[17]

A small group of children known as *provocative victims* may unintentionally invite bullying from others. Many of these children may have an underlying issue, such as attention-deficit/hyperactivity disorder (ADHD) or a learning disability that promotes this unfortunate situation.

The first social need of any human is to be liked. Some children can feel like strangers in kid-land. They don't understand the basic rules of operating in society, and their mistakes are usually unintentional—but often lead to isolation, harassment, and bullying.

Bullies have a strong need for power and control. Bullying is purely about power and about capitalizing on an imbalance of it by intimidating a weaker, more vulnerable child.

One evening, I was about to turn on the news when my daughter, Heather, called to tell me that Silas, her 13-year-old, came home from school crying. He had been attacked and hurt on the school bus that morning.

It was tough at first to reconstruct what happened. My grandson is charming and smart—but not always a great communicator. With Silas, stories tend to veer off in unexpected directions. And Silas, who doesn't cry in front of people, cried in front of Heather, requiring a lot of settling down. This wasn't the first time he had been picked on, and by the time Heather called me, she was sure Silas wasn't making up what had happened on the bus: a boy with whom Silas had a disagreement over a popular song put him in a headlock and punched him in the back of the head.

"I guess he has anger issues," Silas told her.

There was a bloody bruise on the back of his head. Heather had checked.

After settling Silas down, Heather called me, and we discussed how to talk to Silas and, briefly, how to handle the school. So far, the school had done nothing—it hadn't even bothered to send him to the nurse after he showed up to school bleeding from the head.

Heather took Silas to the doctor, both to check for a concussion—he didn't have one—and to document what had happened. A few days went by, during which Heather talked with three assistant principals but never got to the principal herself. One of the assistants told her that district school buses carried video equipment and that he would review the tapes. More time passed, and when the assistant finally got back to Heather, he said that the camera on Silas's bus had somehow failed to record the attack.

I am not only Silas's grandfather but also a court-qualified expert in education law and best practices. For the school district to blow an opportunity to document an assault because a $30 video camera malfunctioned somehow didn't smack of best practices.

In the meantime, at my behest, Heather and Silas had sketched a diagram of where various children were sitting so that they could be interviewed, and wrote a detailed summary of exactly what happened. Peter, the boy who delivered what Silas called "the noggin punch," wasn't someone Silas knew well, but he knew his name. He was two years older than Silas, tall and slender. It wasn't a whodunit.

Heather gave all this information to the school. About a week after the incident, Heather called me, fuming.

"I'm asking, 'What's going to happen to the other child who was in the altercation?'" she cried. "Nothing's happened to him. It's just a dead end. It's, 'Well, there's no videotape; we're done.' Now what?"

Not long thereafter, Heather took Silas out of his middle school—a large, impersonal place in Toms River, New Jersey. He came to live with my wife and me, and we enrolled him at the local public school—one of the tiniest in the state.

It's true that we pulled the trigger quickly in Silas's case; looking out for a kid whose brain chemistry can make his attention wander means extra work for parents—and grandparents. It isn't his fault—Silas is just wired differently. He has a sharp tongue that sometimes interrupts conversations or calls out in class. And not only is he a special-needs kid, he's a powerfully built, brown-skinned young man in an easily threatened white teen world. This wasn't the first time he had been picked on, and it wouldn't be the last. Heather and I wanted to make sure he didn't become one of those kids who is singled out, whose life becomes an ordeal of humiliation.

Dolores and I call Silas "the Panda" because he is so like Po the Panda in the animated movie *Kung Fu Panda*. The panda is clever, brave, and strong—he's a Shaolin master—but hyper. He needs calmer pandas around him. When the disarming, stocky panda, with his slick line of talk and action-hero moves, appeared on the screen in the theater, it was so clearly Silas in bear form that I leaned over to Dolores, mouthed "Silas!" and jerked my finger at the screen. Silas, sitting between us, smiled.

When Silas came to stay with us, we began to understand his vulnerability to bullying. We took him to a specialist who diagnosed him with Asperger's syndrome, a mild form of autism. We already knew he had attention deficit hyperactivity disorder (ADHD). The Toms River school had virtually no programs that met his needs—not even a resource room where learning-disabled kids get extra academic help in a small-group context from a special-education teacher, which is something state and federal regulations require as a special education option. The Toms River school also did not offer one-on-one counseling or social-skills development, both of which are invaluable and commonly available services. The lack of help meant Silas was less likely to fit into the mainstream and more susceptible to bullying.

Resource rooms, counseling, and more were available at his new academic home. But even here, he came in with a strike against him. Teenage boys live and die according to a code of coolness. Cool means being in control, and Silas is often not in control. Words fly out of his mouth with little regard for how they will be received. Prior to the bus incident at Toms River, he somehow got locked inside a locker. There was some confusion as to whether he was shoved in. Silas said he and a group of kids were joking that the lockers were so big "you could fit a person in there," so he jumped into one and couldn't get out.

Silas has been picked on, even attacked, all the way back to elementary school. In a world where fights break out over a comment about someone's sneakers, his disabilities can exacerbate the situation. Dolores and I have learned the hard way that with harassment, especially when children with special needs are involved, there is usually more to the picture than what meets the eye.

Protecting the Panda means understanding that the Panda is a strong personality and that strong personalities inspire both positive and negative emotions. I'm sharing this very personal experience of harassment because I know there are millions of parents in the same boat—one in which a bullying situation is prompted or complicated by the fact that a child is obviously a little different than his peers. Most of us should be able to solve the problem by using the techniques discussed in this book. But sometimes, parents have to start over somewhere else or make a temporary change of habitat for their youngster. Your child is unique—not like anyone else and probably not like the Panda. Knowing your child and understanding what is different about him and perhaps why this difference might be attracting bullies will help you when communicating with the school to seek help for your child—help such as social-skills development. We will talk more about this later when we look at why some kids are bullied more than others.

Intervene early to prevent kids' lives from becoming an ordeal of humiliation.

THE CONSEQUENCES OF BULLYING

Bullying in school is a significant public health problem. Physical aggression has been linked to an increase in injuries, violent crime, school adjustment problems, substance use, and mental health problems among kids. The first U.S. Health Behavior in School-Aged Children (HBSC) survey in 1998[18] identified bullying and victimization as significant problems, and the results prompted an increase in school-based bully-prevention efforts. The 2002[19] and 2006[20] HBSC surveys found significant decreases in bullying activity since the first HBSC survey, providing possible evidence that those interventions are succeeding.

More and more, abuse—sexual and otherwise—takes place online, but the consequences are experienced face-to-face, in real time either at school or immediately after dismissal. When a video appeared on YouTube showing a group of teenage girls in central Florida pummeling another girl, the images spread across the Internet and onto television practically overnight, prompting antibullying bills in Florida, Louisiana, and elsewhere. In the Florida attack, the victim had called some of the girls "slutty" on the Internet. It closely followed incidents in Missouri and New Hampshire in which teens had committed suicide after being publicly humiliated online.

HOW DO YOU KNOW YOUR
CHILD IS BEING BULLIED?

Kids are often loath to tell their parents that they are being bullied, so as parents, we must be observant. The most common indicator that a child is being bullied is a loss of interest in school. A few months ago, your child might have loved going to school and learning new things, but if that has changed, you might have a problem. Because some kids have a hard time expressing anxiety about going to school, it manifests itself in different ways: trying to stay home more often by feigning sickness, expressing interest in dropping out of school, or asking to be homeschooled. Sometimes, the indication might be that your child is just unable to concentrate in school. Poor or falling grades in a particular class might indicate that a problem exists in one class.

Your child might also be losing interest in after-school sports or extracurricular pursuits. The bully could be on the team. Your child might want to leave school as soon as possible to avoid a confrontation. Left unchecked, the bullying might affect his self-esteem, which can make him feel as though he is not good enough for the team or the activity.

WHY DO PARENTS MISS BULLYING?

Most of the time, parents have no idea that their child is being bullied. What is it about bullying that makes it so hard for adults to see— and then do something about it? Student surveys reveal that a low percentage of students believe that adults will help. Students feel that adult intervention is infrequent and ineffective, and that telling adults will only bring more harassment from bullies. Students report that teachers seldom or never talk to their classes about bullying.[21]

Bullies aren't stupid; they hide what they are doing so that they don't get in trouble. Victims hide it because they are embarrassed—and because they worry that talking about it might make things worse (which sometimes happens). Cyberbullying is even harder for adults to see: it's silent, it can happen when the victim is alone, and it occurs within a world and context that most adults don't know about—that is, unless they get up the nerve to ask. Sometimes parents don't want to see it. We all want our children to fit in. It's hard to think about your child being the one who is picked on. Why? Does it bring back memories of your own childhood bullying experiences—times you would just as soon forget? If so, it's tempting to breathe a sigh of relief and take your child at his word when he denies being bullied and says everything is fine—as bullied children often do. In chapter three, you will learn how to find out what's happening with your child by developing and implementing effective communication with him.

Often, parents don't know what to do when they discover that their child is being bullied. Indeed, it can be hard to know what questions to ask, how to ask them, how to react, whether to call the school, and whether to call the bully's parents. We parents grew up in a different era—one in which the consequences of bullying were not well understood and the prevailing attitude was "kids will be kids." Learning how to talk with your child about her experiences can help you determine whether issues you might otherwise barely notice or perceive as trivial are in fact unusual and worth pursuing.

When your child says, "She's making fun of me," "He's picking on me," or "My teacher makes me feel weird," it's easy to chalk it up as a rite of passage. But when your child says, "She's making fun of me *because I have a disability*"—that's disability harassment. "He's picking on me *because I come from a different country*"—that's national origin harassment. "My teacher makes me feel weird *because of how he touches me*"—that's sexual harassment. Chapter three will provide you with a step-by-step approach for getting the facts and the full story from your child.

We all need to fight this together. To make a difference, we need to change the culture of our schools. We need to create a culture that doesn't tolerate bullying. This means education—lots of it—to empower kids to stand up against bullying and to encourage schools to establish clear and consistent consequences for anyone who bullies. It also means giving parents the information they need to turn the outrage of bullying into an opportunity. When you have the same information that school administrators have, you will know how to open the door of the principal's office and communicate effectively to get the school to listen. When you know how to hold a school accountable for its duty to protect our children, change takes place. That's what you will learn how to do in this book.

If your child is doing poorly in school, has difficulty making friends, seems more isolated, or is staying home from school more often, she might have a problem with bullies.

A school, like any other human environment, is the sum of thousands of minute interactions among children, teachers, and staff. The seemingly small act of one child bullying another, if not stopped, is inevitably repeated until it poisons the entire atmosphere. It soon breeds a chain of harms, as communal bonds give way to relationships ruled by distrust and fear. A school that permits a culture of bullying is sending a message that children, not adults, are making the rules. Eventually, you get a negative culture.

Some schools have developed programs aimed at reducing school bullying. However, no policy or program will make a difference unless the school fosters a culture of caring in which administrators and teachers are alert to social circumstances that lend themselves to bullying and act to curtail those circumstances. Research has found that bullying is most likely to occur in schools where there is a lack of adult supervision during breaks, where teachers and students are indifferent to or accept bullying behavior, and where rules against bullying are not consistently enforced.[22]

In those environments, small things lead to big things—sometimes even murder or suicide. Remember that Eric Harris and Dylan Klebold, the teen killers who shot up Columbine High School and slaughtered 13 children before committing suicide, identified with a clique of teens at the school who called themselves the Trench Coat Mafia and whom had been systematically bullied for years by Columbine's athletes, their girlfriends, and the other hangers-on of the ruling "jockocracy." It goes without saying that bullying doesn't excuse mass murder, but if we try to imagine what a bullied child goes through, we might begin to understand the adolescent rage and shame that fueled Columbine. Remember, too, that the brightest kids frequently the most likely to be picked on—don't have thicker skins than other children. Often, the reverse is true. When they go to school authority figures for help and don't get it, the message they perceive is that they must go outside the system for relief. As a result, some kids drop out. Others buy guns and exact revenge. And for a tragic few, the harassment destroys their very will to live.

Victims of bullying experience a range of mental health and social difficulties. These include depression, anxiety, eating disorders, and low self-esteem—all of which can become chronic.[23] In extreme cases, bullying leads its victims to commit suicide. If your child has recently had problems making friends or seems lonelier than normal, a bullying issue may be developing.

Victims also consider school to be an unsafe and unhappy place. Worse, being bullied tends to increase some students' isolation because their friends do not want to hang out with them, lest they risk being bullied themselves.

Take the case of Phoebe Prince. After moving from Ireland to Massachusetts at the age of 15, all Phoebe wanted was to be liked in her new hometown school. As a freshman at South Hadley High, she briefly dated a senior who was a football player. What ensued after their breakup was abuse from the "mean girls" at her school. They stalked Phoebe, called her an "Irish whore," and intimidated her relentlessly.[24] The mean girls followed Phoebe home one day and threw an energy-drink can at her. Phoebe kept walking—past the abuse, past the can, past the white picket fence, and into her house. Then she walked into a closet and hanged herself. Her 12-year-old sister found her body.

Of all the buttons an adolescent can press, none are more powerful than sex and sexuality. As they enter puberty, teens discuss, imagine, and experience sex more intensely than at any other time in their development. In schools, epithets like *fag* or *dyke* are flung about by children who barely understand their meaning. From Oxnard, California, the case of Lawrence King, an eighth grader who was caught up in an escalating cycle of harassment, made the cover of *Newsweek* after a group of classmates mercilessly humiliated King following his public declaration that he was gay. The cycle ended when one of them shot him to death in a computer lab. An adult friend of King told the *New York Times* that King's 14-year-old assassin was "just as much a victim as Lawrence" because "he's a victim of homophobia and hate."[25]

The school district wasn't the one to pull the trigger, but when a child is harassed for any extended period of time, particularly by a group, there is almost always a staff member who is aware of it. It is the school's responsibility to make sexual taunting and gay bashing socially unacceptable. Doing so might well have kept Lawrence King alive and spared his teenage gunman prison.

Like Lawrence King, Stephanie came out—as a bisexual—during eighth grade, which is quite an early age for making a public statement about sexuality. But Stephanie had known she was different as far back as the second grade, when she was diagnosed with ADHD.[26]

"I was quirky and I did my own thing. The kids would mess with you and say, 'We don't want to hang out with you,'" remembers Stephanie, who is now 19.

By the time she started high school, Stephanie knew why she felt so different. Far from hiding her bisexuality, she flaunted it. She wore rainbow pins and jewelry associated with being bisexual. Most importantly, she had a very public relationship with an older girl.

"We were as affectionate as the straight couples. We would kiss by my locker," says Stephanie. "It was really rough because there were no openly gay kids in the school. My female friends didn't get it. My male friends couldn't deal with it."

Others reacted more virulently. Someone broke into Stephanie's locker and scribbled "lesbian" and "dyke" inside of it. Her girlfriend's car was scratched and smashed. Kids made remarks about her in class. A little clique of four girls made it their mission to seek Stephanie out, taunting and threatening her on a daily basis.

With an average attendance of about 350 students, Stephanie's school is the smallest public high school in New Jersey. In larger schools, the staff doesn't see the micro-lives of students; all too often, other priorities draw teachers' attention away from even the children who are harassed on a daily basis. In a small school, on the other hand, there is a greater level of intimacy—the staff knows the students, including their hurts. Harassment is picked up on more quickly. And when that happens, it needs to be addressed. Small, medium, or large, a school needs to create a positive climate. If a school can't turn harassment into a teachable moment, it's not really teaching.

In Stephanie's case, there was simply nowhere for her to hide, and she became a prisoner of her abusers.

"I was a mess. Just in a really bad place," Stephanie says now.

Although she had a supportive circle of friends, Stephanie's staunchest allies were her parents. When Stephanie was suspended for an altercation with another girl, Janet decided her daughter had taken enough. Anxious and frustrated, she came to me for advice.

"You have to make the school understand who Stephanie is and what she's going through," I told her. "I guarantee they don't know she's gay and that this is about her being persecuted for being gay. They think she's some kid who's getting into fights. They want to control her reaction to being harassed rather than really trying to understand what it means for Stephanie to be gay in a small school."

I reminded Janet that it was the school's duty to protect Stephanie from behavior that fits the legal definition of harassment—that is, behavior so severe, pervasive, or persistent that the child can't get the full benefit of a public education. I told Janet that Stephanie's experience fit the legal criteria and that once she made the district aware of what was happening, the district would be breaking the law if the school allowed the abuse to continue.

We decided that Stephanie and Janet should go directly to the superintendent, the top of the district's chain of command. The plan was simple. Bright and personable, Stephanie would tell her story and make the superintendent understand.

The meeting took place a few days later. As she became more comfortable, Stephanie spoke from the heart about her ordeal. At one point, she broke down and cried.

"Everything is being put on me, like it's my fault. But I'm just being who I am," she told the superintendent, who was clearly moved. Even Janet learned things about her daughter she hadn't known. The meeting produced results. The word went out to the four bullies to cease and desist. Stephanie's suspension was rescinded and replaced with a single day of detention.

"Other kids have come out since then and they didn't have to go through what I did," says Stephanie. "The school is pretty gay-friendly now. I'm proud I was the one who broke the barrier."

It is a school's duty to protect students from behavior that fits the legal definition of harassment.

WHAT'S A PARENT TO DO?

There are many red flags to help you figure out whether a school has the kind of disciplinary tone that will keep bullying—which can never be entirely expunged—to a minimum.

Here's what you can do: Call the principal and ask to visit your child in class and to look at the school during school hours. Maybe you already went to the school's open house at the beginning of the school year. But meeting the teachers and seeing the school when no students are there is like trying to swim in a pool with no water. Just as the water makes it a swimming pool, the students make it a school. Get to know the school so you will know how and whom to call if necessary.

Take a walk through the halls during a change of class, or visit the cafeteria at lunchtime. What is your first impression? Is there order and calm, or are students running, shouting, pushing, and shoving? Are teachers visibly present, standing at their classroom doors or directing students in the lunch line? Does the principal stand in plain view to greet the kids in the morning and help them on their way? When you stroll through the playground, do you see three aides huddled in a corner while students throw rocks at each other at the other end of the yard? Is there a climate of respect— one in which teachers respect the students and students respect one another? Your first impressions are usually correct.

A school that doesn't know bullying is happening—or pretends it doesn't know—is not a healthy place for children. Such a school is the kind of place that is highly likely to allow other dangerous conditions to fester. And just as we can perform a spot inspection to help us judge whether a school promotes proper discipline, we can acquire information about a school's potential for other dangers through other windows into that environment.

The chaotic conditions that allow bullies to feel comfortable tend to promote peer-to-peer sexual harassment as well. Is your first grader allowed to go to the boys' room on his own, or does the teacher walk the class to the restroom several times a day so she can supervise who is entering when your child is there? After wrestling practice at your son's high school, how is the locker room supervised? Is the coach in the general area, or does he hang out in his office, unaware that sexual comments are flying in the shower?

Don't be shy about stepping in. Act decisively the first time you feel reasonably certain that your son or daughter is reporting a real incident of harassment. Start by calling or visiting the school and asking for a copy of the school district's antibullying policy. Every district is required to have one (if mandated by the state). If the principal or an assistant gives you the third degree ("Why do you need it?" or "You'd have to have authorization to see that"), that is revealing. It is best to know right away whether the top decision maker in the building welcomes or fears parents who have legitimate concerns. If it's the latter, the odds are good that your next stop will be the superintendent's office.

In chapter four, we'll talk about how to approach the school, how to get the principal's attention, and how the right words and questions will help you enlist the principal as an ally to your cause. You will learn how to get through the layers of administration and get results. When you use all the tools at your disposal but still get no satisfaction, then it may be time to rattle the cages of school administrators and the board of education. In chapter five, you will learn when it is time to go outside the system to obtain the help of cops and lawyers and the attention of the press, as well as when a lawsuit is the best or only option.

When you learn how to communicate effectively with your child's school, you can make things better for your child and for other children. Knowing what the school is supposed to do to protect your child, knowing the policies of the school, and knowing how to communicate effectively with the administration will change everything for your child—I promise. You can be a part of that.

Visit your child's school during school hours. Is there a climate of respect among teachers and students? Your first impressions are usually correct.

If I've learned anything over the course of my career, it's that children and parents can revolutionize the climate in a school, be it public or private; small or large; rural, suburban, or urban. Without question, children and parents are the most important agents for change—positive or negative.

Two quick examples:

The parents at West Windsor-Plainsboro High School are an involved bunch. They email and call. They praise and complain.

And as a result, students and teachers at this New Jersey school have taken it upon themselves to improve the climate.

Consequently, West Windsor-Plainsboro is a model for bully prevention, even though it is a large public high school in which one might expect children to fall through the cracks. Each hallway and area of the school has a designated "safe person" to whom a student who feels threatened can go. Here, the child-inmates are not running the asylum. An adult is watching at all times, and one-on-one interventions are routine.

There are times when a school gets it right. Take the "Ginger Day" attacks in an affluent California middle school. Three boys were arrested after bullying or kicking students with red hair in a prank modeled on an episode of television's *South Park*. On the show, the kids with red hair were singled out for bullying and the day was ceremoniously called "Ginger Day." At the school near Los Angeles, seven students told authorities that they were kicked or pushed. Las Virgenes Unified School District superintendent, Donald Zimring, responded, "Any time a youngster gets hurt because of a thoughtless act . . . there ought to be consequences." This school swiftly organized assemblies to discuss the incident and meted out discipline that ranged from picking up school trash to five-day suspensions. "The youngsters involved understand that this was not acceptable, and they have made various forms of apology and contrition," Zimring said.[27] At an assembly, the principal attempted to demonstrate the irreversible consequences of ill-thought-out actions by having students try to put toothpaste back into a tube using toothpicks. Later, students wrote essays about making the school a better place. This is an example of taking the outrage of harassment and turning it into a teachable moment.

Education means *people changing people*. Imagine what might have happened—or might not have—if there had been that kind of leadership at Columbine, Toms River, South Hadley, and other schools.

Children and parents are the most important agents for change—positive or negative.

Of all the dozens of cases of harassed children I have handled, none had a sadder ending than that of the student leader and the girl in the wheelchair. From this case, we, as parents, can learn a lot about what schools will actually allow—in this case, life-threatening physical attacks and deeply scarring emotional abuse.

Taya Haugstad was adopted from a Calcutta orphanage. Born prematurely after an unsuccessful abortion and dumped in an alley, she was left with severe cerebral palsy, relying on a motorized chair with a joystick to get around. But she fit in perfectly with the close-knit Haugstads in Stanwood, Washington, and their two biological sons. She was an outgoing and joyous little girl.

Daryl was an athletic and aggressive boy. He was handsome, popular, the president of the student council. No one could have foretold that someone like Daryl would harass someone like Taya. But once Daryl developed a taste for it, I could have predicted with absolute certainty—based on my 40 years in education—that he would never stop bullying Taya on his own. The attention from friends and the feeling of power one can get from dominating another can be a thrill that is difficult to give up.

This story begins in the fifth grade, on the playground of an elementary school in a suburb of Seattle, when Daryl, perhaps showing off for his friends, walked up to Taya and called her "a retarded bitch." Taya cried. Nothing happened to Daryl, so he started cursing Taya every time he saw her on the playground until, one day, a playground aide caught him. She made him stand by himself and write out a report—not much of a punishment. Later, when Daryl, a muscular, intimidating child, began to block Taya's wheelchair, she began having nightmares.

"He tries to kill me," she said of her dreams. "He comes at me from the classroom with a gun."

Taya told her mother, Karrie, that she was afraid to go to school. Because of her cerebral palsy, Taya has very limited verbal abilities. Her mother and brothers can understand her high-pitched vocalizations, which sometimes sound like shrieking, but many others cannot. Karrie knew this wasn't helping Taya get the attention of school officials, even though they were obligated to do whatever was necessary to protect her and had specialists on staff who understood Taya's every word. Karrie complained to teachers, playground aides, and the principal, but Daryl's behavior only got worse. Numerous staff members had stern chats with Daryl, but talk was all it was. Daryl's enjoyment of humiliating Taya now came with the added thrill of getting away with it.

And Daryl continued to get off scot-free for the next four years. Taya simply couldn't persuade the school that such a well-respected, popular boy was harassing her. "They all loved him because he was Eddie Haskell," remembered Karrie. "But that was an act. He was really evil." Indeed, Daryl was having so much success hiding his wrongdoing that he felt free to torment a girl with Down syndrome at his church.

Karrie had her daughter repeat the fifth grade so that Taya would not have to attend middle school with Daryl, but that just postponed the inevitable. Thrown together with her again the next year, Daryl not only taunted Taya, he took to yanking on the joystick of her wheelchair so that she crashed or spun in circles. Numerous students and staff members witnessed these and other acts of abuse. Daryl was just a "silly boy," said the director of special education, who said she didn't believe Daryl would do such things. Another parent saw Daryl bullying Taya and reported it to the assistant principal, who told Taya that Daryl was "only teasing" and that she was a big girl and should handle it herself.

"I wanted to cry," Taya told me. But she was determined to try to bull through on her own. She only told her mother about the verbal abuse—not the wheelchair incidents.

By then, an increasingly desperate Karrie had already spoken with more than a dozen school administrators and staff members, including the middle school principal and the district superintendent. She was told it was a "parent problem." Karrie understood the message: *Don't bother us with this. You take care of it.*

Then one day in eighth grade, Daryl grabbed the joystick on Taya's wheelchair, sending her spinning into a wall in the corridor. "My head hit the wall so hard I almost passed out," Taya remembered later. The impact was severe enough that it broke the chair's heavy steel footrest. "That was when I decided my mom needed to know," said Taya, who still cries at the memory.

Karrie called the police, and Daryl was arrested. Karrie got a restraining order prohibiting Daryl from having any contact with her daughter. Only then did the school take disciplinary action against Daryl—a two-day suspension from school and a one-week suspension as class president. The juvenile court required him to do ten hours of community service with the handicapped, skip television for a month, and write Karrie and Taya a letter of apology. (In chapter seven, we will talk about criminal and civil law approaches that are being increasingly used in an attempt to stop school bullies.)

This was all that the system required of Daryl, after Taya had endured a four-year ordeal that left her so badly shaken that to this day, she hears Daryl's voice in her head, calling her "retarded." And in her dreams, he still comes at her with a gun.

And it all could have been prevented that first day on the fifth-grade playground. Unfortunately, playground aides are often the weak link in the chain since they are typically untrained and earn little more than minimum wage. The classroom teachers of both students should have taken decisive action as soon as they knew Taya was being harassed. Daryl could have been kept after school or given an in-school suspension. If the abuse continued—and especially if it escalated to dangerous acts like shoving Taya's wheelchair—Daryl should have been suspended or moved to another school.

The tormenting of a girl in a wheelchair is an outrage. Daryl's classroom teacher could have used Daryl's bullying as a fulcrum to transform Daryl and teach him about empathy. The lessons learned might have changed the direction of his life. A police officer told Daryl's mother upon his arrest, "One of these days you're not going to be there to protect him. And that's going to be a sad day for your son."

When I talk with teachers about bullying, I stress the positive results we can gain from leadership. It doesn't always work, of course, and teachers can't fully compensate for what is lacking in the home environment. But teachers have a professional responsibility to try.

Yet this school district, like so many others will do, sloughed off the danger. Except for her mother, no one bothered to imagine what those years of living hell were like for Taya. And Daryl was repeatedly enabled in a course of behavior that was bad for him and bad for everyone around him. The school wound up on the losing end of a $310,000 lawsuit.

Take the outrage of harassment and turn it into a teachable moment.

Taya's mother knew that what was happening to Taya was wrong. But what she didn't know was that it could have been prevented. She didn't have the tools or the information to know how to do that and, therefore, wasn't as confident as she could have been in attacking the problem. And so, a bad scenario was allowed to play out until the worst happened and Taya was seriously injured by her bully.

In the next chapter, you will learn why you can't count on schools and why you need to have the tools to step in and effectively communicate with the school to get it to listen when your child is bullied. This is the *Bully Action Guide*—use it to take action.

CHAPTER TWO

WHY YOU CAN'T
COUNT ON SCHOOLS

KEYCEPT: Schools are notorious for insulating themselves from the outside world. Overworked and understaffed, principals often don't notice social problems like bullying, even when it's right under their noses. When confronted, administrators tend to agree it's better to keep such unpleasant things under wraps. All too often, schools behave like private companies afraid to tarnish their image. But public schools are public institutions with obligations to those they serve—students, parents, and the community—to be transparent. They have a duty to protect children and to stop bullying. They have a responsibility to give every kid an opportunity to learn in a climate that is free from intimidation, harassment, and bullying. Sadly, schools don't always fulfill these obligations.

Beth Ferry had never experienced anxiety like this before. Like her husband, Beth had been a New York City cop her entire adult life, rising from undercover narcotics duty to the homicide squad, and finally to a highly coveted post in the department's intelligence division. She was among the first law enforcement personnel called to the World Trade Center during the 9/11 attacks.

She had been afraid for her life on the mean streets of Queens. But this was worse. Her 12-year-old son was being beaten and taunted at school on a daily basis. Depressed and listless, afraid to leave the house, Patrick Ferry was on the losing side of a war with a group of mean kids. And although Beth carried a badge and a gun and was responsible for protecting the citizens of New York, there didn't seem to be anything Beth could do to protect her son.

There is nothing worse than feeling helpless in the face of the certain knowledge that your child is being mistreated at school—even for someone as tough and resourceful as Beth Ferry.

Patrick had seemed to look forward to going back to his sixth-grade class at Udall Road Middle School in West Islip, Long Island, after Christmas break. You know only so much about your child's day at school, but what Beth did know was reassuring. Patrick had friends at school, and he looked forward to the bustling socializing in the cafeteria. He was an honor student—always had been. He was polite, he tried hard, he had a generous spirit, and he didn't blindly follow the crowd. He was a good kid—and a happy kid.

Within months, everything was different. Patrick's sleep—when he could sleep at all—was interrupted by nightmares, and he woke up dreading the day ahead. Beth didn't completely understand it. Later, she would realize she couldn't have. She was used to being in control. How could she get inside the head of a little boy whose mind had turned into a video loop of humiliation in which he watched himself being taunted, punched, and kicked?

It started in April when Patrick came home shaking. After a lot of prompting, he eventually told Beth that a boy named Edward had come up to him in gym class, shouted "You faggot," and shoved him. Patrick, a rail-thin, sandy-haired boy, said he had done nothing to provoke the shove.

Beth did what most parents do in that situation.

"Stay away from that kid," she warned him.

But Edward wouldn't stay away from Patrick. And within days, two other boys had teamed up with Edward. They grabbed Patrick's legs, turned him upside down, and dropped him on the floor. Beth Ferry wrote the first of several multipage letters to the principal, detailing incidents of harassment. Patrick was nervous about the letter, and even more nervous about confronting the kids face-to-face. Beth specifically asked the principal not to bring the trio of bullies into the same room with her son. He did it anyway. In the principal's office, Edward and his cohorts formally apologized to Patrick. The very next morning, they brutalized him again.

CULTURE OF SILENCE

Schools are often blind to the pain bullying causes. This mystifies parents, who assume that schools care for the emotional well-being of students because that is the image schools work to project. That's why it takes many months—often longer than necessary—for parents to realize what's happening.

To put it bluntly, administrators are simply oblivious to bullying because there aren't any physical scars; as a result, they dismiss it as harmless tussles between kids. Sometimes, schools try to do the right thing, implementing various responses to bullying—but most miss the mark. Administrators bring in antibullying programs, conduct assemblies with students, talk with teachers about watching out for bullying—but we know that, in spite of these noble efforts of some administrators, bullying is still on the rise. Canned programs will not hold the school accountable for protecting your child from being bullied. Although schools are filled with good, caring teachers and administrators who strive for academic excellence, history shows us that they have been woefully inadequate at protecting our children from bullying.

But you, as a parent, can take the hurt of bullying and place the job of remedying it squarely where it belongs—on the school. Without your intervention, the school is likely to come up with lots of excuses as to why it can't stop bullying—"We don't have enough counselors" or "We don't have the money to hire aides for the playground," to name a couple.

One of the biggest reasons that you can't count on the school to protect your child on its own is that kids don't always appeal for help. All too often, children think that most teachers will not intervene when told about bullying.[1] The school can't respond directly to a bullying situation unless it knows what's happening, so it may not be aware of the extent of bullying within its walls. This is why it's so important for you to know how to communicate effectively with your child and with the school. When you have notified the school that something bad is happening to your child, the school is obligated to respond. (In chapter three, we'll discuss how to talk with your child when you think something is wrong with her. In chapter four, I'll walk you through a step-by-step approach to compel the school to take action.)

In a survey of American middle and high school students, 66 percent of bullying victims believed that school personnel responded poorly when they saw children being bullied.[2] Kids who are bullied often don't tell anyone because they:

- fear retaliation
- feel shame at not being able to stand up for themselves
- think they would not be believed
- don't want to worry their parents
- have no confidence that anything would change as a result

- assume their parents' or teacher's advice would make the problem worse
- are afraid teachers will tell the bully who it was that told on him
- believe it is worse to be considered a "snitch"

It's not just targets of bullying who keep mum. Their peers do, too. Even though most students believe that bullying is wrong, witnesses rarely tell teachers and infrequently intervene on the behalf of the child who is the target of the abuse. In fact, studies suggest that only between 10 and 20 percent of noninvolved students provide any real help when another student is victimized.[3] Students worry that intervening will raise a bully's wrath and make them the next target. They may also feel powerless to do anything about it; after all, they are peers—they are not the teacher, the one in charge of fellow students. So they tend to sit by, watch the negative behavior, feel confused about what to do, and internalize lots of conflicting feelings and emotions.

Students need to know that they are in an environment where they can approach a teacher, the principal, or a counselor with confidence when they are being bullied or see it happening. The school needs to create a climate that communicates unequivocally that it will extend a helping hand and that adults really will help. Quite often, though, this is not the case. And so, parents need to intervene to hold the school accountable for its duty to protect their children.

Phoebe Prince's mother tried as best she knew how. At least twice she talked to school personnel about her daughter being bullied. Moreover, all of the kids knew what was going on, too. And still none of this was enough to get the school to pay attention—until a 15-year-old girl was dead.

The South Hadley school district didn't do enough to save Phoebe's life. Immediately after Phoebe's death, the superintendent defended the actions of school officials, who said they first learned that Phoebe had endured months of relentless harassment only a week before the 15-year-old hanged herself. In the months following Phoebe's death, the school district convened a task force to examine the climate in the school and the administration's response, as well as to make recommendations for programs intended to make the school a safer place for kids. Parents who attended the task force meetings were shocked that "the issue of bullying came as a surprise to many [officials] in the system."[4] Almost everyone knew that Phoebe's mother had been in contact with the school on numerous occasions, so they questioned the level of communication between the principal, assistant principal, and the superintendent of schools. A school official responded by saying that "the teaching staff was not trained . . . to monitor student behavior, but to teach. Our primary resources are invested in education, not in behavior."[5]

In other words, schools don't understand that harassment gets in the way of students' learning experience, whether or not a school has the best teachers in the world. Who can learn when the kid across the classroom is making menacing faces at you?

GOOD INTENTIONS, POOR EXECUTION

In the wake of tragedies like Columbine and dozens of bullying-related suicides, schools have rolled out countless prevention tactics that vary widely in scope and strategy. Specifically, schools have:

- placed greater emphasis on the principal's involvement
- attempted to increase students' reporting of bullying

- provided more oversight for activities in less-supervised areas of the school, such as the playground or hallways
- established monitoring in areas where bullying can be expected, such as in bathrooms and on buses
- educated teachers about effective classroom-management techniques
- trained students in conflict resolution and peer mediation,
- adopted a "zero tolerance" policy
- offered group therapy for bullies
- encouraged victims to stand up to bullies

All of these are well-intentioned, but my years in education have taught me that training bullies in conflict resolution and peer mediation, trying to enforce a "zero tolerance" policy, engaging bullies in group therapy, and urging victims to stand up to bullies don't work.

Teaching kids to resolve conflict on their own is a valuable social skill, but in cases of bullying, it is misguided. Because bullying involves powerful children harassing children with less power (rather than a conflict between peers of relatively equal status), common conflict-resolution strategies or mediation may not be effective. In fact, these actions may actually further victimize a child. Often, bringing the bully and the victim together results in nothing more than the victim later being bullied even more. The harassed kids don't want to meet with the kid who already "has it in for him." Parents whose children have experienced this have told me that this was the worst thing that could have happened to their child. Not only did it aggravate the situation but it caused the child to not go to anyone in the school again for help. This is one reason why you can't count on the school.

So, then, what's wrong with a zero-tolerance policy? Such efforts superimpose a black-and-white approach onto a social issue whose complexity is hidden by many shades of gray. Simply suspending a student for harassing another doesn't get to the root of the bullying behavior, nor does it change the school culture. It doesn't take into consideration an analysis of why the bullying is occurring, where it is occurring, and how the behavior needs to be changed. It only excludes students from the very environment where they are having problems getting along with their peers. They sit at home, often unattended, or roam the community looking for more trouble. This is a shortsighted, ineffective attempt at resolving the problem—and another reason why you can't count on the school.

Group therapy for bullies? Yes, some schools provide self-esteem training for bullies, but this also is misguided. My personal experience—backed by new research into the mind of the bully—suggests that bullies do not lack self-esteem. In fact, most bullies have excellent self-esteem. Bullies usually have a sense of entitlement. What they lack is compassion, impulse control, and social skills. Remember, the act of bullying involves a perceived imbalance of power between bully and target. Bullies get a high from being cruel to others. Some use bullying as an anger-management tool. It's classic sociopathic behavior. Bullies don't need self-esteem—they need empathy.

You can understand, then, why standing up to a bully doesn't work. Telling a student to face down a bully may be physically dangerous for the victim. Yet parents buy into this "get tough" notion all the time—especially parents whose own training has taught them to do the same.

Few antibullying programs implemented in schools have been effective, because most are misguided.

One night, Beth and Patrick Ferry watched a TV show about sharks in which the photographers dumped chum—bloody fish parts—into the water to attract great whites. The smell of the chum drove the sharks into a frenzy in which anything floating near them was devoured. *That's what my son is turning into—chum for bullies,* Beth thought.

It was a month later, and by now, the attacks on Patrick had spread to the halls, the playground, and the bus stop. Kids he didn't even know called him rude words and shoved him into the lockers. "The things they say are worse than getting hit. You can't stop thinking about it," Patrick told his mother.

Beth called Vice Principal Richard Zeitler and asked him to speak directly to Edward's father. Zeitler promised to do so and to let Beth know how it went, but he never called back. She called several more times before she got Zeitler on the phone again.

"He's not interested in cooperating," said Zeitler. Undeterred, Beth kept trying to get Zeitler to arrange a meeting with Edward's parents. "They can't be bothered," he told her.

Weeks went by. Sometimes Patrick came home unusually quiet—almost taciturn. "My kid tells me everything," Beth used to say to her friends, proud that there was no wall of preteen attitude between them. Now she suspected Patrick was keeping the worst to himself. Then one day, Patrick called her cell phone, his voice quavering. He said that he and one of his brothers were riding their bikes near the house when Edward rode up, pulled out his own phone, and said into it, "I'm here with Patrick Ferry and I'm going to beat the crap out of him."

Beth got into her car, roared up on Edward cop-style, and jumped from the vehicle. Edward, in his typical hooligan style, swore at her. Patrick and his brother stared as they stood nearby, balancing their bikes. They were shocked at their mother's actions.

"Why do you want to put your hands on my kid?" she demanded.

"He said he could beat me up, so I was going to beat him up," said Edward.

Beth turned to her son.

"Patrick, do you want to fight this kid?"

"Uh-uh, I don't want to," said Patrick.

She turned to Edward.

"So what's the problem?"

"Hey, I beat him up because I can," said Edward. "Because I feel like it."

"You know what I'm going to do?" said Beth coolly. "I'm going to go get your mother, and I'm going to beat the crap out of her right in front of you, and you're going to watch me beat her up. And every time I see her, I'm going to beat her up."

Beth saw all of the bravado drain out of Edward.

"I don't want you beating up my mother," he said. He began protesting, babbling.

Beth turned on her heel and walked away, letting him think about it. She stopped and turned to Edward.

"You have your mother call me," she said, and drove off.

This is it, she told herself in the car. *Now my son can't even play outside with his brother. This has to stop.* She dialed Zeitler, who said he was too busy to see her.

"OK, then—you have this kid's father call me right now, because I am just done with this," she said.

Zeitler protested that all of this had happened off of school grounds, but Beth would soon learn that the school's disciplinary code mandated that the school follow up on incidents like this. This time, however, Zeitler got Edward Sr. to call.

"I had no idea about this," Edward Sr. said. "I am so, so sorry about what's happened to your son."

Beth was astounded.

"You never talked to anyone at the school about my son? No one from the principal's office ever called you?"

"I would never have allowed this to go on," he said.

Beth's 20 years of experience evaluating witness credibility told her that, indeed, Zeitler had never spoken to him.

"I'm going to straighten him out. I'm the disciplinarian in the house, and this is not acceptable," said Edward Sr.

She told Patrick what had happened and then hugged him. He hugged back and cried with relief. Patrick had no further trouble from Edward. Beth thought she had finally done something that made a difference.

But it took less than a week for Beth to realize that her intervention had not been the cure-all she hoped it would be. The problem worsened. Clearly, Patrick hadn't told her everything. There were several other boys who enjoyed harassing him. Throughout seventh grade, Patrick's life deteriorated. He was beaten on a daily basis. Beth wrote more letters, met with Zeitler and others at the school, and sat through countless infuriatingly ineffective phone calls—all to no avail. The irony was that as a police officer, she felt she could do even less than an ordinary mom.

"I'd just seen it so many times that a cop will step in and because of being a cop, the next thing you know there's an accusation that you used force or threatened someone or pulled a gun, and I just didn't want that for my own family," she remembered later. Frustrated, angry, and unable to defend him, she started to believe that there must be something wrong with how Patrick handled himself. Otherwise, why was he being singled out?

At the end of January 2008, Patrick grudgingly admitted that he was really terrified of one kid in particular—a boy named Brian. Brian was one of the biggest kids in the school—a hulking bruiser who was taller, Beth would later realize, than her own husband. Beth changed tactics with Patrick. Maybe she was being too soft on him.

"You've got to start fighting back," she told him one night. "Somehow, all these kids have the idea you're an easy target." *Don't be chum*, she thought.

It wasn't long before Patrick had the opportunity. One day, when she picked Patrick up after school, she found him trembling, his face and neck bruised. He told Beth how that morning, he was standing just outside the school entrance when Brian approached.

"Get the fuck out of here," Brian said. "You're in my spot."

Patrick moved.

"You're still in my spot," said Brian, shoving Patrick.

"Leave me *alone*," said Patrick, who shoved back.

Patrick fended off the bigger boy as best he could, then ran inside, pursued by Brian, another habitual bully named Ryan, and other boys. The little wolf pack chased Patrick to the end of the hall, then surrounded him. Patrick stood in front of his locker, swinging his backpack wildly to keep them at bay. They were now directly in front of Patrick's homeroom, the door of which was open. Inside, Patrick could hear kids chanting, "Fight, fight, fight," but his homeroom teacher never came outside. One of the kids pushed Patrick down the stairs. He smacked his side and head as he bounced down the steps to the landing. Patrick ran back and swung at one of the kids, bloodying his nose. That stopped the fight.

Patrick told Beth that he went to Zeitler's office, preceded by another child who backed up his account. Zeitler brought in Brian, who apologized. It turned out that Ryan, the other instigator, had just finished a two-month suspension for pulling a knife.

After calming Patrick and getting him home, Beth called Zeitler, who assured her that Brian had been "severely punished." (She learned later, though, that Brian had served only a one-day in-school suspension.) Patrick and his mother had a long talk that night. Beth was at the end of her rope.

Firm adult intervention can stop a single act of bullying from metastasizing into a chain of harms.

WELCOME TO MY WORLD

As a parent, nothing annoyed me more than when the principal promised that she would take care of a concern about my child but did nothing.

As a former school administrator, I know why.

School administrators are very busy people. When I was a principal of an elementary school, I was overwhelmed with improving student scores on state tests; training and evaluating teachers; keeping up on the latest trends in curricula; approving the kindergarten class trip to the zoo; and making sure that students weren't bullied, harassed, or intimidated by fellow students.

If you want to get the principal to listen and resolve your concern, it's useful first to understand the job of the principal and how he or she is responsible for your child.

The principal is the leader of the school. He is like the father, mother, grandfather, or grandmother in your family who is in charge and lets everyone know it. This is a good thing if the power of the position is used for good—which, most often, it is. The principal sets the tone and the climate in the school. When something goes wrong—there's a fight in the cafeteria, the gym teacher doesn't show up for her class, or the field trip bus gets a flat tire—it's the principal who moves into action (or should) because that's his job. He's in charge of everything that happens in the school. The principal works longer hours than anyone else at the school and feels the "weight of the building" on her shoulders. It's a demanding job; answering to the superintendent and the teachers union and tending to all of the other responsibilities can be exhausting and time-consuming.

It doesn't excuse Zeitler for not calling Edward's father sooner, but it gives you an idea of why an administrator might put that phone call on the "to do" list and never get around to it.

That's not to say that the principal is a detached administrator. Just the opposite is true: She was once a teacher and understands the needs of children. A principal generally has an advanced degree in education administration. She is experienced in supervising the staff, approving the lunch menu, disciplining disruptive kids, and hiring the best calculus teacher.

An effective principal doesn't stay cloistered in her office. When she visits classrooms and asks students about their projects, it communicates that adults are interested in what kids are doing and that they care. Good principals also maintain relationships with parents to ensure students' success. This is the person whom parents should contact when their children are being bullied on the playground, when the heat is too high in the science room, or when a child with a disability isn't getting the services she needs.

So why do so many principals give parents little more than lip service? Think about those demands that compete for the principal's time. Calling to complain about something may well ensure that you won't get a call back. With everything else that the principal has to do, who wants to step into the middle of a mess? More than likely, that principal just hopes that you'll go away. But knowing how to get her attention by letting her know that you are an informed parent who first wants to try to work cooperatively with the school to resolve a situation will get the principal to return your call almost every time. I'll tell you how to do this in chapter four.

Beth Ferry knows she made mistakes. Let's look at them.

Looking back, Beth realizes that her own frustration drove her to blame Patrick for his predicament. That is equivalent to telling your child that the bullies are right, that he's a punk who won't stand up for himself, and that he deserves what he gets. And her sadness about her inability to step in and fix it probably made Patrick uneasy and less likely to be candid with her. Beth should have started by just listening to Patrick—listening and asking questions in an atmosphere of calm, not in a fit of emotion. Patrick's feelings—not only as a child but as a child who was being bullied by bigger, more outspoken and powerful kids—were raw and tender. The last thing he needed was for his mother to blame him for what was happening.

Bullying, once it starts, is like an itch that a child has to scratch. The pleasure that comes from intimidating another student is perverse but undeniably addictive to a bully. Most bullies won't stop unless someone stops them. Partly because of her sensitivity to her dual role as mother and cop, Beth was hesitant to use the full range of options at her disposal. She didn't know it, but the school may have been breaking federal and state civil rights laws by looking the other way while Patrick suffered. When a child is treated differently than others in a school—and this can include the school ignoring the fact that the student is being bullied—it can amount to discrimination. When the school knows that your daughter is being bullied yet acts deliberately indifferent to the bullying, causing your daughter to stay out of school to avoid being harassed (thereby missing her right to an education), this might be a violation of the standard set in *Davis v. Monroe County Board of Education,* a 1999 U.S. Supreme Court decision. We will cover this in chapter six. Beth wrote letters to Zeitler about her son's abuse but didn't know that she had the right to climb the education pyramid to protect Patrick—from Zeitler to the principal to the superintendent and right up to the federal Department of Education's Office for Civil Rights, which has the authority to penalize a school that permits a "hostile environment" that inhibits a student from participating in or receiving the benefits of a school's programs.[6] If she feared for her son's safety, she could have called the police months—even a year—earlier.

The pleasure that comes from intimidating others is addictive to a bully. Most bullies won't stop unless someone stops them.

By March 2008, Patrick's grades had taken an uncharacteristic plunge. He was hearing "fag" and "homo" on a daily basis. Beth's sleep became fitful. She bounced from anger to frustration to bewilderment and finally—against her will—to shame. In the back of her mind, she still nursed the thought that Patrick was in some way responsible, that he needed to toughen up.

"Now I look back and I say, I was such an idiot," Beth recalls. "The 'fighting back' thing—how can you beat up a kid who's so much bigger than you? There are three or four of them against you. And once it starts, it multiplies."

Beth admits now that, like most parents, she didn't know whom to talk to at the school district, what to ask for, how hard to push for a solution, or how to counsel her son.

One day near the end of the school year, Patrick got into his mother's car, more upset than she had ever seen him. He told Beth that a boy named Vinnie, who often shoved him around in the locker room during gym, had threatened to kill him the next day. Beth immediately called Zeitler. Zeitler promised to have the gym teacher watch out for Patrick.

"Don't bother getting dressed for gym," Beth told Patrick. "Just stay as far away as you can."

When she picked him up at the end of the day, Patrick was holding a torn piece of a napkin over the back of his head. Vinnie had snuck up behind him as he went out a side door to see his friends after lunch and smashed his head with a rock. The school authorities hadn't sent him to the nurse. In fact, Zeitler had refused to even look at Patrick's head. Beth took Patrick to the hospital, where he was diagnosed with a concussion. And she called the police, who arrested Vinnie. Within days, Beth had hired a lawyer to sue the school. Legally, it was a civil rights lawsuit, but to Beth, it was for allowing her child to be turned into chum, for depriving him of sleep, and for allowing a group of malevolent preteens to do whatever they wanted with him.

Meanwhile, completely on his own, Patrick found a unique way to fight back. While he and his mother waited to see how—or whether—the school would respond, Patrick poured his heart and soul into making a video. It took him a month to complete. He told his own story, but he also did a lot of research on bullying and interlaced images with statistics about harassment, especially about the strong link between bullying and suicide. He bought a video game—a Mortal Kombat–style game of violence in which points are awarded for bullying—and condemned it in his video.

Patrick sent copies of his completed work to the administrators at Udall Road Middle School. By now, the school had dug in its heels, denying any responsibility for what happened to Patrick. They refused to show the video to the student body.

Patrick and his mother talked about what to do next. There was concern about prejudicing the school's response to the lawsuit by embarrassing them publicly. But Beth, as many parents do, became increasingly frustrated with the school—and this turned into anger.

"The hell with it," Beth told Patrick. "Do whatever you want with your video."

Patrick posted it on YouTube where, within a few weeks, it attracted almost one hundred thousand hits. The comments posted by viewers—comments like "It's been only ten weeks of school and I already planned to kill myself"—demonstrated how many children's lives are just as agonizing as Patrick's had become. Their message was that bullying cannot be trivialized as "boys being boys" or overcome with exhortations to "toughen up"—not even for a policewoman's son.

In the end, Patrick's video was a monument to the intelligence and spirit that survives even in a child in torment, and to Patrick's will to find a solution outside of the box.

Bullying cannot be trivialized as "boys being boys" or overcome with exhortations to "toughen up."

A POSTMORTEM

Let's compare what Udall Road authorities did to what they should have done so that we as parents can know what we should expect—versus what a school district may want us to settle for.

WHAT THE SCHOOL DID

Once it knew that Edward and his two cohorts were mistreating Patrick, the school put the bullies in a room with Patrick and forced them to apologize.

WHY THAT WAS WRONG

Bully and victim should never be brought together. An apology in this context is forced and meaningless. Such meetings only retraumatize the victim and almost guarantee that he will be beaten up again for telling on the bully—and that's exactly what happened to Patrick.

WHAT THE SCHOOL SHOULD HAVE DONE

The school should have provided a counselor trained in harassment issues who would have sat down separately with Edward and his friends, and then with Patrick. This was the point at which the cycle of harassment might have been broken, but Udall Road failed to seize it. Any act of bullying is wrong, but it also is an opportunity to do some *real* character education—not in the abstract setting of a classroom but in the actual world of peer-to-peer student interactions.

To not counsel is to take a terrible risk. A child's self-esteem often hangs in the balance. Counseling can help the victim understand that he was not singled out through any fault of his own and that he is not responsible for another kid's pathological need to abuse others. Meanwhile, the counselor uses a combination of reason and emotion to convince the bully that intimidating those who seem physically weaker than he is an act of cowardice, not courage, and to show him in concrete terms how he is harming not only his victim, but also himself.

The school also should have punished Edward and his little gang in a way that would have made it unmistakably clear that such behavior is not tolerated. Detention, in-school suspension, and then varying terms of out-of-school suspension can be appropriate. When all else fails, a student who habitually beats up other children can be expelled. As discipline is meted out, the parents of the offending student should be summoned and told that unless they work with the district to alter their child's behavior, the punishment will escalate. Such an approach might have stopped Edward in his tracks and kept Brian, Ryan, and Vinnie from deciding that humiliating Patrick was just another form of cheap entertainment.

Finally, Udall Road Middle School should have given a standing order that staff members were to intervene forcefully and immediately when a child was mistreated, making it clear that the staff would be held responsible for any consequences. It is telling that only now—in the disgraceful aftermath of the national attention Patrick's case attracted—is West Islip School District thinking of mandating staff training in bullying prevention.

State laws guarantee every public school student a safe and secure environment in which to learn. In addition, West Islip, like every other school district, has regulations fleshing out state laws forbidding harassment and mandating prompt and effective responses to inappropriate behavior. Udall Road shrugged off its legal burden and instead tried to throw a serious bullying problem back into the parents' lap. That is asking for trouble.

Bully and victim should never be brought together. It almost guarantees that the victim will be beaten up again.

I met Patrick and his mother backstage at a TV talk show in New York City. I felt an immediate bond with them. The producer had asked me to appear on stage as an expert in bullying and to answer questions from the parents in the audience. I saw in Patrick not only the similar experiences of the hundreds of children with whom I've worked, but also my own grandson's ordeal—right down to the bloody bruise on his head.

Patrick was accompanied by friends and by one of his brothers. They were his support system throughout the long-term harassment he experienced. Patrick and Beth told their stories. Then I spoke as an education expert about how little the school had done and how badly it had missed the best-practices mark. By its inaction, Udall Road had in effect forged an alliance with the bullies and winked at brutality.

Later, I sat down with the Ferrys and their lawyer to talk more specifically about these issues. And while, legally, it is always up to the school—not the parents—to provide a secure environment for students, I knew Beth had learned some important lessons from her family's yearlong war with the harassers. "There are seven serious offenses in the school code, and Patrick was a victim of five of them, often on multiple occasions," Beth told me.

From then on, I made myself available to Beth and Patrick as they continued to address the hurts they experienced at the hands of an uncaring school administration.

For the record, the district's position was that it had done everything it could. Over the summer, as Patrick made the rounds of national talk shows and his story attracted worldwide attention, the superintendent of West Islip's public schools released a lengthy public statement that concluded as follows: "No situation brought to our attention by either Patrick or his family has ever been ignored. Going forward, the district will continue to explore all viable means to combat bullying in all of our schools and to treat such cases with the utmost seriousness."[7]

Included was a list of antiharassment initiatives, which is worth examining because it is the kind of thing that many districts offer angry parents. These initiatives included an elementary school assembly presentation on bullying; course work in "character education" that covers harassment, among many other topics; and a yearly appearance by a police officer on Internet bullying. Finally, the superintendent pointed out that Udall Road has a chapter of the Friends of Rachel Club. Named after the first child gunned down at Columbine, this support group meets periodically to talk about harassment, providing a safe environment in which students can share their experiences.

"Patrick went, but he stopped when they put a bully in it," Beth told me. This is the equivalent of having a wife beater at a battered women's shelter—not a good way to encourage frightened victims to open up.

Both my own professional experience and studies demonstrate that programs like those offered at Udall Road are either of little value or actually harmful to harassed children. In fact, virtually everything that Udall Road did is a textbook example of what *not* to do. Did the district learn anything from the Ferrys? Perhaps not, but it is worth noting that West Islip demoted Assistant Principal Zeitler a few weeks after the Ferrys filed their lawsuit.

Patrick Ferry did not return the following year to Udall Road Middle School. His parents retired from police work and moved to South Carolina, where Patrick got a fresh start. The last time I checked, he had taken up karate and was going to the beach almost every day with one of his brothers. He also has turned his experience into a cause, working with Love Our Children USA and with the principal at his new school to educate his fellow students about the harms of bullying. There, Patrick organized "Blue Shirt Day," the centerpiece of a weeklong effort at the school to rally the student body to take a stand against bullying. Like "the Panda" in chapter one, being pulled up by the roots did him a lot of good.

This is the extreme and is not easy for most families. In this case, the Ferrys were retiring and already had a place to go to in South Carolina; Patrick's situation just hastened their retirement. When moving as a family or moving your child to live with relatives is not an option, effectively communicating with your child's school can be the solution. You can ask for your child to change classes or for the harassers to be put in different classes to avoid continued problems. You can ask for your child to transfer to another public school within the district or in a neighboring district. If the Ferrys had not decided to move, I would have given them the information to choose other options.

I helped the Ferrys plan their interaction with Patrick's new school before he got there. They took my advice, and he had a very successful first year. Patrick made the honor roll and was a star on the debate team. At the first sign of harassment—and now Patrick and Beth are able to talk with one another about it—Beth knows what to do. She has a copy of the school's antiharassment policy and already talked with the principal when there was the first hint of a problem. Armed with her experience and the knowledge of how to get behind the schoolhouse wall, she was able to effectively protect Patrick from the outrage of harassment and use it as a teachable moment.

If moving your child out of a school is not an option, effective communication with the school can be a solution.

SCHOOLS—ON LAND AND IN WATER

The Ferrys' story, and so many others like it, demonstrates that many parents—through no fault of their own—don't know how to approach school bullying with their children, teachers, or the school administration. It also demonstrates why the school is ineffective and why you can't trust it to do the right thing.

Dolphins swim in groups, or *schools,* to protect themselves. Sharks and killer whales eat dolphins, but by sticking together, the dolphins have a better chance of avoiding trouble. The same is true for school administrators. In South Hadley, where Phoebe Prince was bullied before hanging herself, school administrators circled the wagons, stuck together, and, in essence, said, "We didn't know anything." Yet reports there indicated that at least on one occasion, teachers witnessed the bullying but didn't say anything. When confronted by a saddened and angry community, the superintendent maintained that the school first learned about Phoebe's bullying ordeal only a week before her suicide.[8] At Udall Road Middle School, the administration circled the wagons to fend off the feelings of a very insightful boy who developed a moving video about what it feels like to be bullied.

Like dolphins, school administrators swim tightly together for protection: "Nothing is wrong in our school," they tell themselves. Use this book to get the school to own up to its responsibility to protect your child when you know she is being bullied.

CHAPTER THREE

HOW TO GET THE FACTS

WHAT QUESTIONS
TO ASK YOUR CHILD

KEYCEPT: It's difficult to get your kids to talk about their fears and hurts—especially when they are being bullied. Younger children need your help articulating what's going on with them. Older children often keep their hardships to themselves out of a desire for independence or because they fear retaliation. By setting the right climate—listening, not lecturing— you can find out the facts and help put an end to the bullying.

Lisa was getting harassing phone calls from and enduring harsh verbal encounters with a trio of girls after she broke up with her boyfriend.[1] This is not unusual among high school students who become jealous of another for landing a date with the popular kid; later, when the couple breaks up, the embittered students take it out on their rival by siding with the popular person who was left behind. These situations can get ugly very fast, and with Lisa, it did.

Lisa's parents called the school to complain. They didn't really know the school's internal structure, so they called the principal's office and left a message with the secretary. Their pleas for help went unheard. Whether they ever reached the principal is unclear. Lisa's parents didn't know what to do when their phone calls were not returned. Their daughter was becoming more depressed as the bullies kept bearing down on her psyche. "We're going to get you for dumping John. You wait 'til gym." Then Lisa was shoved into a locker. Nobody saw it happen.

The situation was taking a wrong turn—one that could have caused Lisa to become more depressed—or worse. Lisa's mother felt like she had tried everything. She talked with Lisa, got information from her, and called the school to complain. Still, nothing.

But Lisa's mom didn't have the whole picture. I worked with Lisa's family to construct a complete understanding of what was happening. Once we were able to accomplish that, we moved very quickly to get the school to act. As a result, the school quietly removed the offending trio from the classes and free periods that they shared with Lisa.

STARTING A CONVERSATION WITH YOUR CHILD

The first hurdle in helping to put an end to bullying is to find out what's happening with your child. You need to ascertain the chain of events. Kids are often unwilling to tell their parents that they're being harassed, so as parents, we must be vigilant and sensitive to our children's moods. Don't just dismiss what your child tells you about being called names on the playground as "kids being kids" or simply hope that it will blow over. It may be a symptom of a bigger problem. As we saw in chapter one, changes in behavior or mood can be warning signs of a bullying problem. To unravel that, parents need to ask questions to get information but, at the same time, must create an atmosphere of trust by listening more than talking.

This chapter is about effective communication with your child. We'll cover a step-by-step approach for getting the facts and the full story from a child who is being bullied. You will learn what questions to ask your child, how to document your child's responses, how to create a written record, and how to prepare to approach the school about it. You will also understand why your child's behavior seems so strange at times and learn how to find out what's going on in her very different world so that you can communicate effectively with her.

HOW TO START THE TALK

First, be matter-of-fact and de-emotionalize your encounters. To do otherwise will actually trigger the same feelings the bully evoked in your child: fear, helplessness, and a sense of being overwhelmed by negativity. If you don't think you can do this, it's important to contact a child psychologist or a counselor at the local child health clinic who can.

To understand what *effective communication* can do for you and your child, let's look at what effective communication is and how it differs from just *talking* with your child. Effective communication involves the exchange of thoughts, ideas, and information by using verbal and nonverbal cues so that each person understands—and is able to act on—what has been communicated in a way that seems appropriate or favorable. When you communicate effectively with your child, it develops a foundation of trust because she will sense three things:

1. You are actively listening, which shows that her concerns are being heard.
2. Her thoughts, ideas, and feelings matter.
3. The message you are giving is clear and not punctuated with mixed signals.

If you think your child is being bullied (see the signs of being bullied in chapter one), try to talk with him about it. We'll get into specific questions to ask and techniques to use based on age groups, but here are some basic ideas to keep in mind:

- Stay simple.
- Be brief.
- Be positive.
- Replay the message you hear from your child.
- Make sure your child understands that he does not deserve to be bullied—nobody does.
- Never encourage him to bully back.

The secret to effective communication with your child is to de-emotionalize your encounters.

COMMUNICATING WITH YOUNG CHILDREN

Jason was five years old and already a terror. On the playground, he hit, kicked, and called other kids names. Almost always, his targets were boys and girls who were younger or smaller than he was. Sometimes he told kids that they couldn't play his games. Other times he poked them with sticks. Playground aides tried to do what they could, but time-outs and scoldings didn't change Jason's behavior.

This situation is typical of what happens on preschool playgrounds every day. Whether the issue is repeated incidences of name-calling or acts of physical violence, it is rarely easy to get the full story out of a frightened young child. A six-year-old child has a vocabulary of about five thousand words, while an adult's vocabulary is thirty thousand to sixty thousand words. At this age, a child doesn't have the skills to articulate her problem well. Nonverbal communication, then, becomes an important way of getting your child to tell you what's going on in her world.

Start out by putting your child at ease. Sit at your child's level and maintain eye contact. Ask simple questions that he can understand, using a gentle yet matter-of-fact tone of voice. Listen to what your child says and affirm that you hear him by nodding your head. And try to take note of how he feels when responding to your questions.

When asking questions, try to stick to the facts: who, what, where, when, and how. Starting questions with negatives like "Didn't you," "Don't you," or "Isn't that" confers judgment. Your child needs a sympathetic but neutral conversation partner if you're going to get the story from him.

You want to know who did what and who was around to see what happened. Get times, dates, and places. Be as precise as you can. Here are some questions to ask:

- What kids were there?
- Was there a teacher who saw what happened?
- Who was the kid who called you names or hurt you?
- Whose class is he in?
- Where did this happen?
- When did it happen?
- What, exactly, did the kid say to you?
- What, exactly, did the kid do to you?
- Is this the only time that this happened?
- What other times did it happen?
- Did this person do anything else to you?

You might find that it's hard for your child to talk and that he doesn't respond well to direct questioning. In that case, instead of asking him outright if he is being bullied, ask questions about his day, whom he likes best and least, and how he feels about certain classmates. Don't push the issue if he isn't willing to talk. Making him reexperience something that is upsetting can make for a demoralizing conversation, and your child will need your calm support—not a challenging interchange that can only add more anxiety to the situation.

Listen to the answers—don't judge or respond to any of them. Give your child the space to express herself and get it all out. (This can be very difficult, especially for teens who are asserting their independence and don't usually confide in parents. We'll talk more about teens later in this chapter.) Don't tell your child that she is wrong or that he started it all by wearing that weird shirt to school.

After hugs and encouragement, talk with your child about why some people are bullies. Decide what information you will share with your child about bullying, and share it at a level that she can understand. You can talk, for instance, about why some kids bully others: they may be angry about something else, they may not know how to get attention in a positive way, they may want to show off, or they may push your child's buttons to try to get a reaction.

Talk with your child about ways to end the bullying. Talk about whom she can go to in the school to report bullying and who else in the school can help her. We'll be talking more about who might be some key people in the school and how they can help your child in chapter four. Try discussing with your child the options that she may have for dealing with bullying behavior. You might be surprised at some of the solutions she might envision on her own. Try some of them—they might work!

Listen—don't judge. Try to get the facts by asking who, what, where, when, and how.

COMMUNICATING WITH TWEENS

Remember Taya, the wheelchair-bound middle school girl in chapter one who was harassed and bullied by Daryl until her mother, Karrie, called the police? Karrie complained to teachers, playground aides, and the principal, but she didn't know the extent of Daryl's cruel behavior. Taya told her mother about the verbal abuse she endured, but not that Daryl delighted in yanking on the joystick of her wheelchair so that she spun in circles. Karrie learned of it only after Daryl sent Taya crashing into a wall.

Let's look at what Karrie could have done to learn what was happening so that she could have made Daryl stop bullying Taya before involving the police.

First, she needed to have a conversation—probably a series of conversations—with her daughter to produce a more complete picture of what was happening at school. We think we know our children, but what happens behind the closed doors of the school for 35 hours a week is too often a mystery. Don't assume that you're getting the whole story simply because your child begins to talk about bullying. Sometimes the worst is simply too much for her to acknowledge. It may take time and special effort—perhaps an afternoon spent together doing some favorite activity instead of a face-to-face talk over a table—to pry loose the whole truth. A child's friends may also be a valuable source of information. In this case, Taya's friends knew more than Karrie.

Middle schoolers are more articulate than youngsters. And though they start challenging their parents at this age, most are still open to discussion—unlike high schoolers, who often assert their independence through a lack of communication with parents. This means that many middle schoolers are willing to share their feelings with their parents. They want to be heard. By now, they have developed shared values with their friends and a sense of social justice. They understand right from wrong but haven't yet learned to sort out the shades of gray. They are still malleable and are open to parents' guidance.

Again, the trick is to ask questions, listen, and be nonjudgmental. Here are some questions to ask your middle school–age child about bullying:

- Who did you sit next to at lunch today?
- How was the bus ride home?
- I notice that you don't like going to school on Thursdays. What happens on that day that you don't like?
- Are there a lot of cliques at school? What do you think about the kids in these cliques?
- What do your teachers tell you about bullying in school?
- Are kids allowed to bully in school?
- Is there someone in school who makes you feel bad?
- Is there someone in your class who is physically hurting you?
- Who did you play (or "hang out") with today?
- What did you play (or "do") at recess?
- Did you like playing?
- Would you have liked to play with someone else or play different games?
- Is there anyone you don't like at school?
- Tell me why you don't like that person.
- Are you looking forward to going to school tomorrow?

Keep in mind that at this age, your child chooses friends for very different reasons than he did when he was six. Because the relationships are deeper, he won't want to lose face with his friends. If a bully says to him, "Are you gonna tell your mommy?" in front of his friends, chances are he won't talk to you without being prompted.

Sometimes it will take more than one conversation in a nonthreatening environment to pry loose the truth from your child.

COMMUNICATING WITH TEENAGERS

Lisa's mother was becoming distraught, angry, and domineering— both one-on-one with her daughter and when she met with me. Sometimes, parents have to bring in an outside counselor, an emotional neutral, to get to the bottom of their child's downward spiral. Here, I played the role of calm questioner and was the only one who could get Lisa to talk about what was happening to her.

In front of her parents, Lisa talked about being frightened by her old boyfriend and his three friends. She told her mother and father that these girls were calling her names she wouldn't want to repeat in front of them. But because I was asking her the questions, she was able to tell me directly. Clearly, the way her parents were communicating with Lisa and the way they were trying to communicate with the school were not helping the situation. Things needed to change! The spring needed to be unwound. I was able to get the facts from Lisa by asking the right questions the right way.

When I met with the whole family at my office, I quickly realized that I needed to take control, redirect the conversation, organize ideas, structure questions to Lisa, and set in motion a plan of action that the parents would implement with the school to stop the hurt. I knew Lisa's parents would be able to do this if they got a little direction in a calm, rational atmosphere.

The questions that I asked Lisa went deeper into her emotional state than questions for younger children might, but the tone was still matter-of-fact and nonjudgmental. You can adapt these questions to your own child's situation.

The first several questions were aimed at understanding what was happening to Lisa and who else knew about it:

- What's happening at school?
- Are there kids making you feel bad at school?
- What are they doing to make you feel bad?
- Why do you think they are doing this to you?
- Tell me more about that.
- Where is this happening?
- What is happening in school and what is happening outside of school?
- Is this happening in any particular class?
- Who is the teacher in that class?
- Does the teacher see what's going on?
- Tell me what the teacher saw in his class.
- Do these kids treat you this way outside of class?
- Where does this happen?
- Is there a teacher who sees this happening?
- Did you talk with anyone at school about any of this?
- Whom did you talk to?
- What did you tell that person?
- What did she say she would do about it?
- Did you notice any change after you talked with her?

I then tried to learn something about the culture in Lisa's school by asking her these questions:

- Do you know what the school's antibullying policy is?
- What's your understanding of it?
- Does anyone at the school tell the students that they are not to bully?
- Who tells them this?
- Did you ever have an assembly at school to cover bullying?

Finally, to break down the communication barriers between Lisa and her parents, I asked her questions designed to get her to think about how her parents could help in a constructive way:

- What do you want your parents to do?
- If they do this, how will that change things in school?
- Will things get worse or better?

During my discussion with Lisa (and it was a discussion, not an interrogation), her mother attempted to butt in and answer for her. I didn't let her. Lisa needed the space to tell her story to someone who would really listen and not interrupt or interpret for her. Lisa was very brave—she answered all of my questions, and we talked about her very sad feelings in front of her parents, who were hearing some of these feelings for the very first time. Not only did I get the information that I could now put into a letter to the school, but Lisa felt good that someone was listening to her.

By the way, when I asked Lisa what her parents should do, she said, "They can't do anything." Having already enlisted her as an ally by allowing her to speak, I sought to bridge the communication gap with her parents. "Lisa, tonight we're going to work at this.

We're going to put a plan together for your parents, so they will be able to end the bullying. They'll know exactly what to do. Can we work on that?"

She gave me a very quiet "OK."

In chapter four, we'll talk about how I took all this information, put it in a letter to the school to be signed by Lisa's parents, and got a meeting with ten school personnel—including the superintendent and school lawyer—within three days. At the meeting, the school took effective action, and the bullying ended.

What Lisa's parents did was effectively communicate with the school—and the school realized that her parents knew what they were talking about. When the school got the letter, someone took out the antibullying policy and read it. The school quickly realized that Lisa's parents had read it and that the school was in trouble because it wasn't being implemented. The school could have reassigned students to separate Lisa from her bullies, but it hadn't.

At the meeting, not admitting they were wrong, the administrators offered to change the offending students' class schedule so that they would no longer be in Lisa's classes and have less of an opportunity to bully her. The school also offered Lisa the opportunity to report to a teacher of her choice any instances of future bullying. She picked her favorite teacher, one whom she trusted. Lisa was also given an opportunity to spend time with her counselor, who dealt with the impact of the bullying on her emotions and her schoolwork. When the new school year started, the bullies were out of her classes and the school set up the support system. She never had to use the support system, though, because simply not being in the same class as her tormentors made all the difference.

About a month into the new school year and a successful change at the school, I received a handwritten thank-you note from Lisa:

To Dr. Dragan,

I want to thank you so much for everything you have done for my family and me. Dr. Dragan, you made me feel comfortable and important when I needed to explain my situation. It is so hard to be a victim and not feel like anyone is listening to you, but besides my family, you listened to what I felt and I appreciate that more than words can express. I'm so very thankful for all that you have done to ensure my safety at school.

Lisa

I received a Christmas card later that year from her family with this postscript: "Lisa is having a good senior year! Thank you again."

Teens may lose faith in your ability to help if they think you are not listening or bringing your own judgments into the conversation.

THE TEENAGE BRAIN: A WORK IN PROGRESS

I worked with a mother who noticed that her teenager's grades were going down; the teen was also beginning to ask to stay home from school.

"What's wrong?" she would inquire.

"Nothing," came the reply.

Of course something was wrong. As we saw in chapter one, falling grades and rising absences are just two warning signs that your child might be in a bullying situation.

One of the reasons teenagers don't report bullying is humiliation. Older children report bullying less often than younger children because they are often embarrassed and fear retaliation.

What's the difference in mind-set between younger kids and teenagers? The brain! Not long ago, we thought that the brain was fully formed by the end of childhood. But research over the past decade has shown that adolescence is a time of profound brain growth and change. Between childhood and adulthood, the brain's wiring diagram becomes more complex and more efficient, especially in the brain's prefrontal cortex. This is the part of the brain that is responsible for impulse control, judgment, decision making, planning, and organizing. Changes that are involved in other functions, like emotion, also occur in adolescence. And the changes keep coming, right through college and into adulthood; this area of the brain does not reach full maturity until around age 25!

As a parent and an adult, your response to stimuli tends to be more intellectual. But a teen's response is often more from the gut. This explains why unintentional injuries are the leading cause of death among adolescents.

So as parents, we need to recognize that when we are dealing with teenagers, we are dealing with a completely different brain— one going through changes that make it very different than the earlier one and the later one. How can this person who gets good grades in school, who is the captain of the chess club, and who volunteers at the local nursing home be the same person who rearends a car while texting her friend? Responsible and reckless at the same time! Who is this kid? Why does she do that? What can I do? And how can I find out if she's being bullied?

"The teenage brain is not just an adult brain with fewer miles on it," says Frances E. Jensen, a professor of neurology at Children's Hospital Boston. "It's a paradoxical time of development. These are people with very sharp brains, but they're not quite sure what to do with them."[2]

Powered by technology such as functional magnetic resonance imaging, research has revealed that young brains have fast-growing synapses, as well as sections that remain unconnected. This allows teens to be easily influenced by their environment and prone to impulsive behavior, even without the impact of stepped-up hormones or any genetic or family predispositions. Teenagers think and act differently. This information has profound implications for how we teach, communicate with, and discipline this age group.

Research also demonstrates what every parent can confirm: the teenage brain is not easily reckoned with when it comes to communicating about bullying.

Things can often become worse when we, as adults, apply adult solutions to a teen's world. His world isn't the same, and we adults don't usually understand that. Encouraging your kid to buck up—"Stand up to that kid," "You are bigger," "Don't let him call you names"—is the product of an adult perspective. It's too simplistic, and it doesn't work for your child or any other child. When you say something like this, you put the problem back on your child. Then, when it doesn't work—and it won't—he will feel even more defeated and blame himself for not being able to handle the situation. He doesn't have to handle it himself. Never communicate to your child that he is to blame for being a victim.

According to psychologist David Walsh, former president and founder of the National Institute on Media and the Family, and author of the 2004 book *Why Do They Act That Way: A Guide to the Adolescent Brain for You and Your Teen,* "The fact is that the teenage brain is built for power struggles."[3] What does this mean for you and your teen? Encourage her not to enter into a power struggle with a bully. And you should be careful to avoid becoming trapped in a power struggle when trying to communicate with her about bullying.

In calm situations, teenagers can rationalize almost as well as adults. But stress seriously affects decision making. The frontal lobes help put the brakes on a desire for thrills and taking risks—a building block of adolescence—but they're also one of the last areas of the brain to develop fully.

"Thinking strategies change with age," Sarah-Jayne Blakemore, a psychologist at the University College London Institute of Cognitive Neuroscience, reported at a 2006 scientific conference in Norwich, Great Britain.[4] "As you get older, you use more or less the same brain network to make decisions about your actions as you did when you were a teenager, but the crucial difference is that the distribution of that brain activity shifts from the back of the brain [when you are a teenager] to the front [when you are an adult]."[5]

Blakemore studied teens and adults, asking how they would respond to specific situations. As they did, their brains were imaged.

"We think that a teenager's judgment of what they would do in a given situation is driven by the simple question: 'What would I do?'" Blakemore said at the conference. "Adults, on the other hand, ask, 'What would I do, given how I would feel and given how the people around me would feel as a result of my actions?'"[6] The changes in brain structure that influence these kinds of behaviors do not happen gradually as a child grows older; they occur in spurts—most profoundly during puberty.

What does all of this mean to you when your teenager is being bullied?

It means that your child doesn't think like you do. She can't reason that if her dad talks with the school, and the school handles the situation carefully, the bullying will stop. So, then, how do you communicate with your teenager when you suspect she is being bullied at school? How do you get her to understand that you are there to help and that the school is there to protect her?

Be careful in communicating with your teen. You want to develop a partnership with her. The way you talk with her can demonstrate to her that you have the ability to communicate effectively with the school to stop the bullying. If you can't effectively communicate with your child, she will reason that you can't possibly effectively communicate with her school.

Here are some questions that will shut down communication with your teen:

- "How was your day?" Teens don't welcome questions like "How was school?" or "How was the dance last night?" Don't expect to hear anything more than "Fine" in response. These are surefire questions to end a conversation before it begins!
- "Why don't you just tell that bully to leave you alone?" The teen brain doesn't know how to do this effectively. Your kid needs help with this. Teens need to be taught safe strategies to fend off bullies so that they're not the target of more bullying.
- "Why don't you just forget about it and let it go?" This isn't practical. A child bullied is a child hurt emotionally. Their hurt is strong, and they feel it deeply. Remember, a teen isn't likely to come to you about being bullied because she is embarrassed and ashamed about it.

Develop a partnership with your teenager through careful communication.

TIPS FOR GETTING INFORMATION

How could Lisa's mom have handled communication with Lisa differently?

First, she needed to compose herself and be calm. She wasn't giving Lisa any room to talk without being interrupted. Lisa didn't need that from her mother. She was already feeling dominated and intimidated by the kids at school—not that her mother meant to make Lisa feel even worse. After all, she was just trying her best to protect Lisa. As parents, we all do that. But Lisa was being closed in on two sides—by the mean girls and by her well-intentioned mom.

Lisa's mom had some of the information about what was happening at school but not everything. She knew that a group of kids were tormenting Lisa, but she didn't know exactly what they were saying to her. Because Lisa didn't share the details until our meeting, her mom didn't know where this was happening; who witnessed it; or anything about the school's policy against bullying, harassment, and intimidation. Once we got together, her mom realized that her idea of how to deal with the school was skewed by her passion for Lisa's well-being. She learned that her own interactions with Lisa made it difficult for Lisa to be completely open and to trust that she would do the right thing with the school to end the bullying.

Stopping the outrage of bullying starts with effective communication with your child, whatever her age. That's how you can elicit the full story, make her feel that she is not to blame, and develop strategies that work so that the responsibility of ending the harassment is placed on the school. This is what happened in Lisa's case. You can do the same.

Doing so requires some thought, effort, and discipline on your part. Before talking with your child, prepare yourself. Consider how you are going to handle her questions and emotions—as well as your own. Some of the following ideas are age appropriate, and some are universal:

- Above all, detach emotionally. Staying calm will help you gather the information you need.
- Be as nonjudgmental as possible. There won't be a reason to hold back if your child senses that you won't accuse her of starting the bullying, won't punish her for fighting back, or won't ask her, "What did you do to get her angry at you?"
- Use open-ended questions. If you use a question that begins with *why*, you are setting up a confrontational climate that will cause your child to be defensive.
- Don't use yes-or-no questions—they won't get you much of a response. Use questions that will stimulate conversation between you and your child. "What did you notice about Sophia today at the party?" works better than "Do you like Sophia?"
- Reflect back what you're hearing: "Oh, you didn't like the way Sophia played with you." Then you can add, "How did she play?" "What feelings do you have about her?" This will give you even more information.
- Don't try too hard to get your child to talk. The harder you try, the more he'll resist you. When you relax the pressure a bit, he'll sense it and be more ready to talk to you.
- Remember that it may take more than one conversation to get the full story. Your child may feel like telling you only so much the first time through. A second conversation when both of you are refreshed gives you a chance to think of follow-up questions that will elicit more information.
- Try using the car as your "office." You're in a small space with no distractions, and it's already a place where your child has spent many hours with you before.
- Get involved in a physical activity that your child enjoys. Playing a game of catch, riding a bike, or shooting baskets

loosens the endorphins and could be the key to setting a relaxing tone for your child to get talking.

- Talk with her while she is coloring, working on a puzzle, or playing with a dollhouse or a favorite toy. When you use these times to allow your child to express herself, she is more likely to express herself to you as well. When you get down on the floor with your child, join her in the activity, and let her talk, there's a lot you can find out.

- Slow down and be available. As parents, it's not unusual for us to miss what's going on in our children's lives because of the hectic pace of our own. If you're not available, your child will turn to alternative means to deal with the frustration and hurt of being bullied. Many of these alternatives—self-medication, to name one—may compound the problem. You need to be there when your child needs you the most.

- Listen. Some kids can be long-winded, and their stories can lack continuity, but let them tell it. After all, it's their story— so let them go on. Listen, engage, and learn.

Just as there are methods for getting your child to open up to you, there are some slam-dunk ways to turn your child off. Here are just a few:

- allowing siblings to interrupt
- allowing your child to be distracted by the television
- allowing yourself to be distracted by the telephone, your BlackBerry, or something going on in the house
- rushing the conversation and not focusing on your child's feelings

- interrupting when he is trying to talk
- being dismissive by saying things like "You're being too sensitive" or "Come on—did he really do that to you?"
- giving meaningless reassurances like "This will pass over," "I'm sure your teacher will take care of it," or "Everyone gets bullied—even I did when I was in school"

Give your child your undivided attention. Give her time and space to tell her story.

WHEN YOU HAVE THE INFORMATION

Carefully document the information you get from your child. Write everything down. Develop a story of what happened and what's still happening with a time line. Then, review it with your child to be sure that you have all of the relevant details.

Here's a list of what to do next:

- Ask your child for a copy of her "agenda" or school calendar, which often includes the district's antiharassment policy and disciplinary code of conduct. I have developed a model antiharassment policy and student discipline code of conduct (see appendix). See how it compares with what you get from your school.
- Check to see if you have a copy of a parent handbook sent by the school. Some schools provide these for parents at the beginning of the school year. Many make them available online. Check what the school is telling you about its antiharassment policy and see how it compares with the model in the appendix.

- Have your child keep a log or diary of what is happening to her at school. If she is too young to do this herself, talk with her each day and write down the important events.
- Use the log and information you obtained from talks with your child to put together a narrative of what has been happening with him. This should be simple and to the point, detailed with names, dates, incidents, who saw what, and what sort of response—if any—there was from school personnel.
- Practice telling the story back to your child and check to be sure it's accurate.
- Practice telling the story to a trusted friend to get feedback on how you are explaining the details.

The school is responsible for protecting your child from harm—the physical and emotional harm that results from bullying. But as we have seen, the school can't be counted on to protect your child. You need to know how to communicate effectively with your child and then with the school to end the bullying. In chapter four, we'll talk about how to use the information you just got from your child when you contact the school.

The right to protection in school is more powerful than the bullies. Getting the school's cooperation starts with getting your child's full story.

HOW TO APPROACH THE SCHOOL

KEYCEPT: To most parents, schools can be intimidating. Making that first call to the principal about your child being bullied can be scary—after all, when you were a student, you wanted to steer clear of the principal's office at all costs. Crazy though it may sound, parents often avoid involving the principal in their child's bullying. But with a record of facts, a script to follow, and careful planning, you will have the confidence to communicate effectively with the principal and put an end to the bullying.

In chapter three, you learned how to communicate effectively with your child to get the facts and to develop a script of what's happening. Now you will learn what to do with that information and how to communicate effectively with the school. After reading this chapter, you will have a script for a telephone conversation with the teacher and one for the principal. You will know how to get behind the administrative veil to get the school to do what it is legally supposed to do—stop the bullying and protect your child from harm.

All children are entitled to be educated in an environment that is welcoming and to be treated with respect by staff and other children. After all, how would you feel at your job if one of the people you work with was constantly sneering at you or calling you by an ethnic slur? You probably wouldn't be able to concentrate on your work, affecting your productivity and maybe even your chances for a raise or a promotion. The same happens with your child in school when she is subjected to negative behavior from other kids.

Most educators do take their responsibility to stop bullying very seriously. But the school often needs a nudge from you—and sometimes more than a nudge—because as we have seen, you can't always count on the school to act on its own.

Not reporting bullying to the school puts the burden of dealing with it on the child. That responsibility belongs with the school.

TALKING WITH THE TEACHER

You might think that talking with your child's teacher is a good idea—and it might be in some circumstances if the bullying is taking place in that teacher's class and nowhere else in the school. Talking with the teacher notifies him that you are aware of what is happening and that he needs to pay attention and respond.

Keep in mind that it is very unlikely that the harassment your child endures is limited to a single classroom setting. Think about the playground, the bus, the lunchroom—does your child come into contact with the same kids in those places? If so, the principal is the person to approach. As the leader of the school, the principal has the responsibility to ensure that school policies are being implemented to create a positive climate for learning. She is responsible for making sure the teachers are protecting your child from harm and has a duty to train teachers in antibullying techniques. Sometimes, talking with the teacher—especially when the teacher might be the bully (which we will cover later in this chapter)—can make it worse.

That's not to say that you should never talk with the teacher. But there may be times when the quickest route to action is to place the responsibility squarely where it belongs—on the school administration.

If you want to try talking with the teacher first, here are a few suggestions:

- Ask if she ever suspected that your child was being bullied. If she answers yes, then ask when she noticed it, what she noticed, and where it was happening.
- Then ask, "Can you let me know if this happens again?"
- Follow this with the question, "What did you do to stop the bullying?"
- Tell the teacher what your child described. This is where you use the script you developed from your conversations with your child (see chapter three).
- Ask the teacher if she has noticed what your child described to you. If she says yes, ask what she did to stop it.
- Ask the teacher to tell you what will happen next. Get an action plan. What will the teacher do if Ray calls Sam a "fag" and pushes him on the ground at recess? Write it all down.
- Set up a time to call the teacher back to review this again and to discuss what she did to end the bullying. Don't let any more than five school days go by!
- Send the teacher a thank-you note. In the note, list all of the things that you discussed and review the action plan that you and she developed.

If nothing gets better after the calls with your child's teacher (or multiple teachers if your child is in junior or senior high school), a call to the principal is the next step.

An effective principal maintains relationships with parents. If your child comes home a week after you talked with the teacher and says, "Mommy, the bullying got worse," the principal is the person you should call.

WHAT NOT TO DO

Lisa's parents were frustrated, angry, and exhausted from trying to get the school to do what it should have been doing—protecting their daughter from the torture of the mean girls. Lisa and her younger sister sat quietly at the conference room table as their mother broke into Lisa's story and talked and talked.

"I couldn't believe that her friends could be so mean to her. I called the school counselor, and she said she met with Lisa and that she just has to toughen up. 'These kids will stop and go away after a while,' she told me. 'This is kid stuff.'"

Well, it didn't go away—it got worse. After no success with the counselor, Lisa's mother finally dialed the principal so that she could arrange a meeting with her.

"Ms. Martine[1] won't be available to meet with you. Can she return your call?" the administrative assistant responded.

"No, I really need to come into the school and see her right now," said Lisa's mother. "My daughter is coming home crying. There are kids being mean to her, and I want it stopped."

"I'll tell her, and she'll talk with Lisa about it."

"Lisa already talked with Ms. Foster,[2] her counselor, but I don't know what to do—I don't know how to stop this."

"I'll let Ms. Martine know."

Feeling hamstrung and livid, Lisa's mother hung up. Would she ever penetrate the sanctuary of the principal's office? Would Ms. Martine ever call back? How long would Lisa have to endure such pain?

Two weeks went by, and there was no meeting—not even a call from the principal.

Schools don't respond to these types of calls from parents. Only when Lisa's parents learned how to communicate effectively with the school did they get a meeting with the principal, superintendent, counselor, two teachers, and the school board attorney—within three days. We'll see how they accomplished that later in this chapter, but first, a lesson in School Administration 101.

Let's imagine that you do reach the principal and get this response:

"Thanks for letting me know that Kiel teased Madison on the playground today. I'll talk with Kiel about it."

Is this an empty promise? It very well might be, depending on how you presented the issue. One thing that would cause me, as a principal, to change my focus from my busy day would be when a parent calls about a concern and has the right words, the right questions, and the right attitude. I would listen, and I would act.

Knowing this, how should you bring a concern to a principal so that you can have it resolved?

THE RIGHT WORDS

The best way to get the administrative assistant to say, "The principal isn't available right now" is for you to call the school and exclaim, "I have a complaint, and I want to talk to Mr. Williams right now!" Part of an administrative assistant's job is to run interference for the principal, and most likely in this case, Mr. Williams would not be "available" at that moment. He might consider returning that parent's call within the next day or more—if at all. After all, who would voluntarily step into a confrontation?

Here's a different idea: Call and introduce yourself to the administrative assistant as the mother of Madison who is in Mrs. Gibbs's class. Ask if she would be kind enough to send you a copy of the playground policy, and ask how many people are out there supervising when your daughter goes to the playground. (A sample letter to the superintendent to request policies can be found in the appendix.) Next, ask if you can set up a telephone conference with Mr. Williams when he's available to talk about the playground. Let the administrative assistant check the principal's calendar and set up a time for you to call when he's not caught off guard or distracted by other priorities. This sets a much better tone—one that allows Mr. Williams to gather his thoughts about the playground, set the time aside, and instruct his administrative assistant that he is not to be disturbed when you call.

Using the right words makes all the difference. Some words are confrontational and will surely cause a negative reaction. Don't demand to talk with the principal "this instant." Avoid using phrases like *I want, I have a complaint, right now,* or *he/she better.* When the listener is already on the defensive, she's not really going to listen. Instead, set the stage for your concerns to be resolved.

Using the right words makes all the difference. Phrases like this instant, I have a complaint, *or* he/she better *put the listener on the defensive—and cause her to stop listening.*

THE RIGHT QUESTIONS

By building a relationship with the principal on the basis of mutual respect and concern for your child's well-being, you can help to make the school more responsive to your child's problems. You are much more likely to enlist the principal as an ally than to turn him into an adversary if, during the teleconference, you demonstrate the same tact and cooperative spirit that got you on his calendar. Remember, the goal is to end the bullying—not to pick a fight.

A checklist for the teleconference starts with calling on time. That sounds simple, but the principal is busy. Punctuality shows that you respect the principal's time and that you appreciate his willingness to share some of it with you. Use the same tone with the principal as you used with the secretary and have the script that you developed from talking with your child (see chapter three) to help yourself stay focused. Introduce yourself and tell the principal that you were reading the playground policy and have a question. This is your opportunity to tell the story of what happened to your child. Be factual, not emotional. Ask the principal how you can work together with him to make things better for your daughter and other kids on the playground.

Ask some of the same questions that you asked the administrative assistant. If you are concerned about bullying in the cafeteria and you asked the administrative assistant to send you the student supervision policy that covers lunchtime, ask the principal if you received the right policy. Ask if there are other procedures or if there is additional information not covered in the policy that you should know about. Ask who is in charge in the cafeteria, on the playground, on the school bus, or wherever your child is being bullied. Ask whether the person in charge was trained in dealing with bullying.

It's important that you write down everything that was discussed in the call. All too often, we lose track of what was discussed and what promises were made. You should finish the conversation by repeating what you and the principal will do together. Sending a thank-you note to the principal after the call, summarizing the conversation and action items for follow-up, notifies the principal that you are watching the situation and that you expect steps to be taken to end the bullying.

Here's a sample script. With some word substitution, it can be effective in almost any situation:

PARENT: Hello, Mr. Williams. This is Madison Lubick's mother. She's in Mr. Kauffman's seventh-grade class. I really appreciate your taking time out of your busy day to talk with me.

PRINCIPAL: No problem, Ms. Lubick. I know Madison. She's a very nice girl. I saw her just this morning in gym. What can I do for you?

PARENT: I was reading the school's playground policy, and I have a question.

PRINCIPAL: What question is that?

PARENT: Actually, a few questions. How many kids are out on the playground when Madison's class is there? And how many teachers are outside with them?

PRINCIPAL: Let's see. At that time—fifth period—there are 178 students on the playground and two teacher assistants.

PARENT: Do you think it's possible for the teacher assistants to watch all the kids at the same time?

PRINCIPAL: Well, they try to do their best. With the budget cuts, we can't afford any more assistants, and the teachers union prohibits teachers from supervising kids at that time.

PARENT: I just wanted you to know that I have a concern about the level of supervision on the playground and whether the assistants are really watching the kids. My daughter was pushed by Ray and John from another class. She fell, cut her leg, and had to go to the nurse. This happened before, and I think she's being bullied.

PRINCIPAL: I'm sorry. I didn't know she was hurt. Who were the students again?

PARENT: Ray and John, from Ms. Finegold's class. What can you and I do together to help the situation so that Madison isn't pushed and hurt by them again?

What makes this script effective? Common courtesies, for starters. Ms. Lubick showed respect for the principal's time: *I really appreciate your taking time out of your busy day to talk with me.* She showed Mr. Williams that she made an effort to become informed before calling: *I was reading the school's playground policy, and I have a question.* She didn't put Mr. Williams on the defensive: *Do you think it's possible for the teacher assistants to watch all the kids at the same time?*—a far more effective conversation builder than *Don't you think that's not enough supervision?* She firmly asked for help with a cooperative spirit, not a demand: *What can you and I do together to help the situation so that Madison isn't pushed and hurt by them again?*

Beyond civility, this script is effective because Ms. Lubick did her homework and worked to extract a promise of help from the principal. She told Mr. Williams that she knows the school's playground supervision policy. She now knows how many students and teacher assistants were on the playground. She informed Mr. Williams that she knows who injured her child and that her child was sent to the school nurse. She asked him to do something so that Madison wouldn't get hurt again. Ms. Lubick should write down Mr. Williams's response, and if she doesn't get a commitment from him to do something—such as discipline the students involved, talk with the teacher assistants about better supervision, or speak with the seventh grade about playground behavior—then she should write that down, too.

A thank-you note to Mr. Williams repeating the main points of the meeting and his commitment to resolve the issue gives Ms. Lubick the documentation she needs to get action. Sending a copy to the superintendent—his boss—also effectively puts everyone on notice: the school knows about the concern and promised to resolve it.

A thank-you note summarizing the conversation and action items for follow-up notifies the principal that the parent is watching the situation and expects a resolution.

THE RIGHT ATTITUDE

I never talked with a parent who yelled at my administrative assistant. I never called back a parent who demanded I call right away. On the other hand, I always called back the one who complimented me on a program in the school but also had a question about how I or a teacher was handling a concern she had.

The three keys to getting cooperation from the principal are as follows:

1. *Understand the role of the principal.* He's the leader of the school and can make changes.
2. *Use the right words to get in the door.* Don't be confrontational—it won't resolve your concern.

3. *Ask the right questions to get information.* Knowledge is power. The more you know about how the school works, the more success you will have in ending the bullying.

By applying these principles, you will have the right attitude when bringing a concern to the administration. Displaying an attitude of cooperation gives the principal an opportunity to use her training and skill as the school leader. The right attitude enables you to open the door to the principal's office, bring in your concern, get a commitment for intervention, and hold the administration accountable for ending the bullying.

WHAT TO EXPECT AFTER THE CALL

After you talk with the principal, here is what you should expect to happen—and what should not happen:

THE SCHOOL SHOULD INVESTIGATE RIGHT AWAY

The school does this by talking with the teachers, watching the kids around your child, talking with other kids indirectly about what they are seeing, and talking with your child discreetly. Meeting with your son to learn about the bullying he has experienced, who is involved, and what policies and school discipline codes are being violated is the first step for the principal or the person assigned. Most importantly, the staff should develop a plan to keep your child safe and should be extra watchful for any future bullying episodes.

SCHOOL LEADERS SHOULD REASSURE YOUR CHILD

The principal, counselor, or social worker should promise your child that he will be watching carefully to make sure that the bullying does not continue. Also, it's important at this stage for the principal or designated person to assure your child that the bully will not know that she told on him, as allowing this to happen is an unproductive approach—it often leads to more bullying when the bully finds out that your child is a snitch. It's better when the school follows through by watching closely and by letting students know that they are being watched. This, in itself, can stop the bullying. It can also provide an opportunity for an administrator or other staff personnel to observe the bullying taking place and intervene without the bully knowing that your child tipped him off.

"BULLIES, REPORT TO THE OFFICE"? ABSOLUTELY NOT!

Some educators meet directly with children who are suspected of bullying. *This is never a good idea.* These kids will figure out who told on them and will make it worse for their target. If the principal says, "I know that some of you are bullying Michael, and I want it stopped," you can be sure that Michael will be bullied on his way home that day. Nor should the principal tell these students that Michael ratted them out. If the principal or another administrator has seen the bullying taking place, she only needs to let them know that they are being watched and to remind them of the rules and consequences of their behavior.

NO JOINT MEETINGS

Similarly, school staff should never arrange a meeting between your child and the child who bullied her. This could be embarrassing and intimidating for you child. The school should also not refer them to mediation. Bullying is a form of victimization, not a conflict that might be solved through mediation. Bullying cannot be mediated.

SWIFT ACTION IS WARRANTED IN SOME CIRCUMSTANCES

When it is obvious who was bullied and who did the bullying—like in the incident with Taya and the fifth-grade class president—then the school needs to act quickly to implement its student code of conduct. This might mean suspending the bully. Although this might have some unpleasant repercussions for your child, the school must do this to show consistency and protect itself from charges of discrimination. The school must treat all students according to its student code of conduct.

PROFESSIONAL HELP MAY BE NECESSARY

In some circumstances, your child should be scheduled to see the school counselor or social worker to work through the bullying issues. It's important that you and the school avoid making your child feel like he is at fault for being bullied. Your child is the victim. Remember why some kids are bullied more than others? It could stem from a lack of social skills that tends to make them magnets for bullies. Some of the students who are bullying your child could be reacting out of annoyance toward his behavior, as was the case with the Panda in chapter one. That doesn't make it right, of course, but it may mean that your child might do well to learn social skills, to be less impulsive, or to draw less attention to himself. This is a good time for him to see the school counselor and for you to explore outside services that specialize in social-skills development for children.

GIVE IT TIME, BUT NOT TOO MUCH

What is a reasonable amount of time for the school to investigate and learn what has been going on? It might take as long as a week or more for the school to gather information and to respond to your concerns. Give the school time, but not more than a week. Schools don't always respond the way we parents would like, so you want to keep your concern on the front burner. When following up with the principal, use the same tact that you displayed during the initial meeting with him. But you need to be firm, direct, and businesslike. The principal knows that you are an informed parent—one with power. This can be intimidating to the principal, so he'll want to do his best to keep the issue of bullying from his boss. Although it's never a good idea to threaten to take it to the next level, just asking for the phone number of the superintendent's office will be enough.

KNOW HOW TO ACT RESPONSIBLY

As a parent, you want your child's suffering to end, but it's not your place to tell the principal how to run her school, how to investigate the bullying, or how to approach the bullies to end the hurt. It's your job to bring the issue to the school in a very organized and rational manner: communicate effectively with your child, get the facts, write a script, learn the school's policies, talk with the teacher, watch for change, contact the principal, get a commitment for an action plan, and see if anything changes. And if it doesn't, there's more that you can do. We'll cover that in the next two chapters.

A school's investigation should follow its antibullying policy, which will be modeled on state laws governing the prevention of student harassment in schools. If a school's investigation appears to be going nowhere or seems to be taking an undue amount of time, it may be that the school has not been enforcing its own antibullying policy. You might be surprised how many school districts develop policies to comply with state law and then let them collect dust.

DOES YOUR CHILD'S SCHOOL MEASURE UP?

When Lisa's parents called me about their frustration with the high school's lack of action, I quickly realized that the school wasn't implementing its antibullying policy. Their state, New Jersey, has a comprehensive antibullying law that, like all state-level antibullying laws, outlines the broad components that every school district in the state must include in an antibullying policy. New Jersey's law defines bullying, requires each school district to adopt a policy that compels school employees to report incidents of bullying, outlines a procedure for investigating reports of such behavior, and defines consequences for engaging in bullying.

In Lisa's case, procedures for reporting, investigating, and disciplining clearly weren't being followed. Lisa's teacher referred her to her counselor, the principal wasn't responding to messages that her mother left with the administrative assistant, and nothing was happening to the kids who were mistreating Lisa. Once Lisa's parents learned what was happening to their daughter and what the school's policy said should be happening in response, they were able to write a well-crafted letter that forced the school to take the policy off of the shelf, dust it off, and read it. Not only did school officials read it, they actually applied it—and ended Lisa's bullying.

Most states have laws that require school districts to develop and enforce policies prohibiting bullying, harassment, and intimidation. Each state law is a little different and, often, was crafted in response to incidents that were prevalent in that state. Take, for example, the law in Massachusetts. It specifically requires anyone in the school to report to the principal any observed incidents of bullying. It also addresses cyberbullying. Those two elements were in the mix when Phoebe Prince hanged herself after numerous students relentlessly harassed her: some of the trauma she endured was allegedly witnessed by school staff who did not report it, and Phoebe was belittled and bullied on the Internet—even after her death.

When you know that your state has a law requiring schools to have antibullying policies, you can hold the school to everything the law and local school policy require. But just having a policy doesn't give the school any points in the "good school" category. Many schools have policies that do little more than gather mold until someone finds out what it says and holds the school accountable for its implementation.

Most antibullying laws require school boards to include information about how bullying will be handled in their schools' codes of student conduct. Most state laws say that school policies must do the following:

- They must allow students, parents, or school staff to report acts of bullying in or out of school to teachers and school staff (some state laws require reporting). The policies must also allow for the anonymous reporting of bullying incidents.

- They must require school personnel to investigate all reports of bullying filed by students, parents, guardians, or school staff and develop an intervention strategy for school staff to deal with bullying.

- They must require the creation of a process that includes contacting the parents or guardians of bullies and the children who are being bullied. The notification must include a description of what the school staff will do in response to the bullying and what the consequences will be if there is more bullying. Schools must also maintain a list of the number of verified acts of bullying in school and make the list available.

- They must require the creation of a mediation strategy that involves counseling and intervention, and that addresses repeated incidents of bullying against a single child or by the same child.

You can get a copy of your state's antibullying law by visiting www.bullypolice.com. You might be surprised by what you find; most state laws are fairly comprehensive. When you look up the law, compare it with the policy you got from your child's school. You are now an informed parent who knows the state law and the policy of your child's school. You now have all of the tools you need to make the school put an end to the bullying: you know how to communicate effectively with your child and the school, you have a script, and now you will be able to put the facts together and hold the school accountable for your child's safety.

Schools should investigate your report right away, in step with state laws and the school's antibullying policy. Give the school time, but not too much—follow up in a week.

DEALING WITH PRIVATE SCHOOLS

Putting a child in a private school in the hopes that this will stave off harassment is usually misguided. We may think that in exchange for paying a hefty tab, we get more control over our child's environment; that private institutions are a refuge from the harsher world of public education; or, at the very least, that the headmaster will take our complaints seriously. Precisely the opposite is often true. Parents usually have less control at a private institution.

"I saw Mr. Nonesuch rubbing my son's back," says the parent.

"How awful! Boy, that doesn't sound like Mr. Nonesuch, though," replies the headmaster. "Fortunately, we can live without your tuition. And you know, I'm not sure your son really fits in here. So good luck finding another school."

After spending tens of thousands of dollars on a private education, many parents are shocked to discover how coldly they are treated when they report bullying, sexual abuse, or other serious problems. Private schools are allergic to negative attention and prone to burying dirty laundry. And because private schools don't get federal or state money—which is what gives the government the right to enforce regulations in public schools—parents have no right to much of anything from a private school's administration.

What strategies can you use to be effective with a private school's governing board? Methods for dealing with private schools differ considerably from those used to get cooperation from public and charter schools, which are publically funded.

- Review the contract you have with the private school to see what it promised about protecting your child from bullying.
- Review the marketing material from the school. Does it promise that children will learn in a safe environment?
- Use all of the other strategies from this chapter when communicating with your child's teacher and principal or headmaster.
- Send a letter directly to the head of the school's board of directors if you are not satisfied with the results.

Although the private school is not mandated to educate your child as a public school is, often the private school will respond to the

economics of the tuition check you write. This is the difference between public and private schools.

A script for a phone call with the private school principal or
headmaster and a sample letter on harassment to the principal or
headmaster, as well as a letter to the private school board of directors, can be found in the appendix.

If you have given the process time to work but the harassment
continues, it may be time to take your child somewhere else, go to
the police, or even sue the school. How do you know when it's time
to take these measures?

If the principal or headmaster has the attitude that there are
plenty of kids waiting to get into the school so they don't need your
tuition, you know you're in for hitting the stone wall.

If your child was physically injured by another student in the
school, you can go to the police. If you feel that the private school
did not meet its promise with you in the tuition contract or its
promise in the marketing material, you can sue for return of tuition. Detailed information about involving the police and lawyers
can be found in chapter six.

---

*If you feel that the private school did not meet its promise
in the tuition contract or in its marketing material, you
can sue for return of tuition.*

WHEN THE SCHOOL IS THE BULLY

Darek was a fifth-grade outcast. Less than a year after 9/11, Darek,
a Muslim, was harassed by his classmates at the overwhelmingly
white Eagle Ridge Elementary School in Douglas County, Colorado.

"Go back to your own country, terrorist," kids shouted at him.

Darek was not one of the more spectacular students at Eagle Ridge—his grades were mostly Bs and some Cs. He had blots on his disciplinary record, but they were trivial—scratching his name in wet cement on the playground and getting into a snowball fight. So other than his ethnicity, I could find no good reason why this ten-year-old was arrested, expelled from Eagle Ridge, and transferred to another school after a girl claimed that he threatened to bring guns to a park near the school to help assault a student.

A crying fifth grader named Joseph was ushered into the office of Ms. Truglio, principal of Eagle Ridge Elementary School. Eagle Ridge is next door to Littleton, where the Columbine High School massacre had taken place just three years earlier.

From the beginning—as is often true with schoolchildren—it was a case of something someone said they heard someone say about somebody else. Joseph told Truglio that Darek said a boy named Dage threatened "to shoot Joseph with a BB gun or hit him with a bat."

Truglio interviewed another fifth grader, who said that Dage "was going to shoot Joseph five times in the head with a pistol" after school but that Dage later decided that he would attack Joseph with a bat. Darek told Truglio that Dage talked only of using a bat. Dage denied everything.

No one mentioned Darek as a perpetrator. It seemed that Darek—along with several other boys—was guilty only of spreading a rumor. The threat never materialized into action. And it almost certainly wouldn't have now that school authorities had entered the picture.

It was only the next day that the principal's "investigation" turned up three girls, one of whom claimed that Darek said that he planned to bring guns to a nearby park to help Dage attack Joseph. The other two girls had slightly different stories or got their information from the first girl, Julia.

But another set of facts put the friction between the boys into perspective—and explained why the girls implicated Darek. It turned out that Dage was angry with Joseph because Dage liked Julia and Joseph made Julia cry on the playground. It also happened that the three girls who accused Darek hated him and evidently took an opportunity to get him into real trouble by capitalizing on his ethnicity, the pervasive suspicion about Muslims, and the volatility of a gun-related threat.

Truglio's handwritten notes clearly showed the direction that she had chosen: "Zero tolerance for threats." "Police situation."

She made a lengthy statement to the Douglas County Sheriff's Department implicating Dage and Darek in a plot to shoot Joseph, never mentioning Dage and Joseph's conflict over Julia—or the girls' possible prejudice against Darek. This was an unforgivable error in judgment. No one knows better than an elementary school principal that fifth graders will make things up about classmates to get back at them for some imagined hurt. A second look at the facts should have convinced her that she was being manipulated.

A sheriff's deputy called Darek's parents at 2:00 A.M. to ask whether they had guns—which they didn't. The next day, Darek and his parents were summoned to school, where Darek was arrested and charged with harassment and menacing. He was suspended for ten days, then expelled and put in another school as a "habitual offender" because of his disciplinary record.

An elementary school principal should know that kids make things up about classmates to get back at them about some imagined hurt. If your child's school acts against your child without getting the whole story, it, too, is engaging in bullying behavior.

HOW TO APPROACH THE SCHOOL

Shortly after 9/11, then-secretary of education Rod Paige found it necessary to write a letter to school officials around the country. Prompted by numerous incidents of harassment and violence against schoolchildren perceived to be of Middle Eastern origin, Paige reminded administrators of their duty under Title VI of the Civil Rights Act. That statute holds schools responsible for providing students with an environment free from discrimination and harassment on the basis of race, religion, color, or national origin.

That didn't protect Darek, who was disciplined more severely than others for the same offense—spreading a rumor—because he was of Middle Eastern descent. In Darek's case, his parents might have seen red flags when Darek previously was written up for fairly harmless school-yard behavior. A phone call or a letter questioning such relatively heavy-handed punishment would have been advisable. Once the school clearly showed its hand by yanking Darek out of class on flimsy and contradictory evidence, his parents needed to not only write a letter documenting why this was wrong, but also probably go over the heads of the local school officials for a more sympathetic reaction.

What can you as a parent do if your child comes home with a story of this type of harassment? What can you do if your child is disciplined more severely than another kid with a different personal background for the same offense—or disciplined more harshly than the school's own rules allow? Children who are targeted in this way face profound educational, emotional, and physical consequences.

When the school is the bully and you suspect that your child is being treated unfairly and in a discriminatory manner, the steps to effective communication are the same as if your child were being bullied by a classmate:

- Talk with your child about what is happening, using the guide in chapter three.
- Get the school's antibullying policies. Also get a copy of the student code of discipline.
- Review what your child is saying that he did against the code of discipline to determine whether the punishment fits. If it doesn't, your child might be a victim of discrimination—a form of bullying that comes from the school, not a fellow student.
- Put your script together and call the principal's office to set up a telephone conference.
- Review, with the principal, the student code of conduct and ask for a copy of the discipline report that was completed on your child.
- Compare the discipline report against the principal's description of the student code of conduct to determine how or whether the behavior fits the code of conduct.
- Send a thank-you letter to the principal and a copy to the superintendent. In the note, repeat what the principal described as the rule of conduct that your child violated and what the punishment was for it.
- Take note of whether the response from the school follows the code of conduct. If not, point that out in the letter and ask for an explanation. Here, you are documenting that you reviewed the code of conduct, that you read the school's allegations about your child's behavior, and that you are questioning the punishment.

There might be mitigating circumstances that caused your child's behavior on that day. Take the story of third-grader Leon, for example. When Leon's mother called the school, very upset because he had been given a three-day in-school suspension for telling a class-mate to "go to hell," she thought that his behavior might have been the result of pent-up anxiety over the fact that his father had just suffered a heart attack over the weekend. (By the way, it's a good idea to let the teacher know when something of that magnitude happens at home if it's likely to affect your child's behavior.)

When Leon's mother called the principal, she had her script ready—she had talked with her son and got the facts. She heard from him that two boys were teasing him about his lunch that day. Leon was in his own world, sad and worried about his father—would he ever see his father happy again?—and these kids were trying to shake him out of it by taunting him. Leon had enough, held up his fists, and yelled at them—"Go to hell!" When the teacher aide heard this, she immediately told Leon's teacher, who wasn't even there. The teacher, in turn, applied the school's student code of conduct—Thou shalt not curse!—and wrote him up for cursing and sent the slip to Ms. Decker, the principal. Ms. Decker, in turn, called Leon to the office and curtly applied a three-day in-school suspension for his outburst of frustration.

What just happened here? The principal, like in the classic telephone game we used to play as kids, received the information at the end of the line and didn't know—or even ask—what might have caused the outburst. The discipline was meted out according to a "zero tolerance" approach. That's not zero tolerance for the behavior—that's zero tolerance for finding out what might have caused Leon's behavior. The result? A young child was bullied by the school.

When this happens to your child, you can follow the questioning techniques that you learned in chapter three and the tips that you learned in this chapter for dealing with school administrators to end the bullying.

If the bullying continues, you will need to take it up a notch. If the school does not respond or your child continues to be hurt after you have notified the school, the school is breaching its duty to protect your child. In chapter five, you will learn what recourse you have: how to take your concerns up the chain of command, how to be persistent, and how to be a calm force in your child's life to hold the school accountable. In chapter six, you will learn when and how to involve law enforcement and when to consider a lawsuit against the school if your child continues to be injured physically and/or emotionally.

WHAT TO DO WHEN YOU GET NO RESULTS

KEYCEPT: As a parent, you act in the best interests of your child. Yet you can work only with what you know. Most parents have access to only a limited amount of information that can help them interact effectively with their children's school. Knowing what school administrators know—and knowing what administrators are responsible for doing—gives you an edge and the ability to stop the bullying. But if the bullying continues after you've talked with the principal, you can take the situation further within the school system—and beyond.

School officials in the small community of Saranac Lake, New York, began their review of school harassment and bullying policies after a firestorm erupted over an incident involving a 12-year-old black student in a mostly white school. The girl's backpack was ransacked after she left it outside her middle school. Students reportedly used the deodorant stick in her backpack to scrawl a racial slur on a school sidewalk. It took the school more than a week to remove the graffiti—not because it couldn't have been done right away. They just didn't get around to it. The local media reported that this was just the latest in a chain of harassing incidents, including the existence of a MySpace page that kids used to taunt the girl for her skin color and leave aggressive and offensive notes—some that encouraged her to commit suicide.

Saranac Lake Central School District superintendent Gerald Goldman said officials were looking toward a systemic solution through all levels of school interaction—from the hallways to classroom curricula—to prevent bullying and prejudice in Saranac Lake schools.

In an open letter apologizing to the community for allowing the situation to linger, Goldman and the president and vice president of the board of education spelled out their starting point:

> No child should fear attending our schools, riding our buses, walking our halls, and playing on our playgrounds. No child should be hated, harassed, and bullied because of their race, religion, or for any other difference. . . . We will examine and revise how we teach tolerance and diversity to our children. We will work with our staff to make certain that all children are valued and that no child comes to school afraid.[1]

The superintendent's public statement and his involvement in addressing bullying in school really made a difference. In comparing schools with high and low bullying rates, research suggests that a principal's personal involvement in preventing and controlling bullying is decisive in lowering rates.[2] The Saranac Lake youngster had, according to published reports, endured racial harassment for a year before the backpack incident got school officials' attention. Goldman acknowledged that that should not have happened and asked parents to help so that "this pattern of hatred [does not] define our schools."[3]

This is all good. But in the moment—when your child is being hurt by bullying—it doesn't mean anything to you.

You met with the principal, using the script you developed after talking with your child (see chapter three). The principal reassured you—"Don't worry. We'll watch your daughter, and we'll talk with the kids who are bullying her." You sent the principal a thank-you letter, reiterating how he promised to do this (see chapter four). But a week later, your child is intimidated by a group of ninth graders who told her she had better not try out for the cheerleading squad. These are the same students who called your child a slut and pushed her into the wall. You did everything to stop the bullying, but nothing has changed. Maybe now it is even worse.

Now what do you do?

You need to go up a level in the school system to the superintendent and, if nothing changes still, to the board of education. Following the steps I outlined in the last chapter, you sent a copy of your thank-you letter to the superintendent—the principal's boss—informing him about the extent of the bullying and what the principal told you he would do about it. Now, the superintendent is on notice. He will not be caught off guard when you contact his office to ask to speak with him about the bullying that hasn't stopped.

As principal of a kindergarten-to-eighth-grade school, I was responsible for knowing the policies of the school and developing a school climate that was welcoming and that provided an opportunity for all students to learn and grow. Because this was a relatively small school (425 students), I was the only administrator—both principal and superintendent. When a parent had an issue with the way I handled a discipline problem with her child, she called a school board member to complain, and I heard about it from the board president that day. The communication was swift and often unpleasant for me to hear. After all, who really wants to be criticized?

As you know from chapter two, the principal juggles many responsibilities and is prone to tuning out some things that you may consider important—that is, until you communicate effectively with him. When the board president called me about anything, it got my attention. You might need to do the same to get the principal's attention—and to make the school follow through on its duty to protect your child from harm.

TAKING YOUR CONCERN TO THE SUPERINTENDENT

If the thought of approaching the principal once seemed intimidating to you, the idea of approaching his boss might seem even more unnerving. Even the principal would rather not hear from the superintendent! But by applying the skills you have developed through this reading, you can be confident in your ability to get the superintendent's attention—and his commitment to act.

In chapter four, you learned how to communicate effectively with the principal, using the right words, the right questions, and the right attitude. You want to use this same approach with the superintendent. The difference, at this stage, is in the message: two weeks have passed since you spoke with the principal and your child is still being bullied.

When you talk with the superintendent, use the same tact you used in your conversation with the principal. It will make all the difference in securing his cooperation. Using the example from chapter four, imagine you are Madison's mother, who spoke with the principal about her daughter being bullied by two boys on the playground.

Start by letting the superintendent know who you are, and say that you believe he received a copy of the letter that you sent to the principal. Briefly review your child's situation, as you did in your discussion with the principal, but try not to labor over it; a quick review to set the context will do. The superintendent's time is limited, and you want to get to your point—a request for his help—quickly.

Mention what the principal told you he would do to end the bullying. If the principal said, for instance, that the counselor would make time to talk with Madison, the superintendent will know this because that was in your thank-you letter. Next, go through each "action item" in the letter and let the superintendent know what has taken place and what has not. Remember, as with the principal, you don't want to be confrontational—you want to build an alliance with the school. Here's a sample script. With some word substitution, it can be effective in almost any situation:

PARENT: Hello, Mr. Kennedy. This is Madison Lubick's mother. She's in Mr. Kauffman's seventh-grade class. I really appreciate your taking time out of your busy day to talk with me.

SUPERINTENDENT: No problem, Ms. Lubick. I have a copy of the letter that you sent to Mr. Williams over at Madison's school. I see that you already met with him about what's going on with your daughter. How can I help you?

PARENT: Yes, I met with Mr. Williams two weeks ago, and as you can see in my letter, he told me that Madison would have time to talk with her counselor, Ms. Stevens, about how she's feeling about being bullied by those boys. But this never happened. She told me that she never met with Ms. Stevens and that the bullying is still going on.

SUPERINTENDENT: I'll talk with Mr. Williams about that and make sure it's set up.

PARENT: Just yesterday, Madison was pushed and tripped again by Ray and John from Ms. Finegold's class. Mr. Williams said that he would go into the class and review the antibullying policy with everyone. I don't know if that happened because they are still bullying Madison. I know that the school's antibullying policy says that if any student bullies another, he or she will receive an in-school suspension. Did that ever happen with Ray or John?

SUPERINTENDENT: I don't know if they were seen bullying Madison or if they received in-school suspension. I'll have to check that out with Mr. Williams.

PARENT: Thank you for listening and for following up. You know, Madison's grades are now being affected because of the bullying. In fact, now she's talking about not going to school. She especially hates going to science class. I think that's one of the classes where the boys are with her. When can I expect to hear from you?

What makes this script effective? Like with the principal, you showed respect for the superintendent's time: *I really appreciate your taking time out of your busy day to talk with me.* You showed that you made an effort to resolve the situation through Mr. Williams. You followed the proper chain of command—the principal first, then the superintendent. The superintendent already knew that you were an informed parent and had received a promise from Mr. Williams to follow through, because in your thank-you letter, you mentioned the school's antibullying policy and summarized Mr. Williams's commitment to do something to end the bullying. Now, you are telling the superintendent that after two weeks—a reasonable amount of time—the bullying has not ended and what Mr. Williams promised has not been fulfilled.

Perhaps equally important—if not more so, from the superintendent's point of view—is that you have made it clear that because
the bullying did not stop after the school was made aware of it,
Madison's education is at risk: *Her grades are now being affected. In
fact, now she's talking about not going to school.* If this isn't corrected,
it can have serious legal consequences for the school district. (We
will talk about that in chapter six.)

Just as you did after your meeting with the principal, send a
thank-you letter to the superintendent repeating the main points
of your conversation with him and his commitment to resolve the
issue. This time, send a copy to the principal. The principal will
not want the superintendent to know that he promised something
that was not delivered. He especially won't want his boss to know
that because he didn't follow through by enforcing school policy,
your child doesn't want to go to school. The idea, of course, isn't to
make the principal uneasy; it's to get someone's attention in a way
that will end the bullying. Making the superintendent aware that
the principal knows your child is being bullied, that the principal
said he would intervene to stop it, and that it's still going on should

---

*The keys to getting cooperation from the superintendent
are similar to those you followed for the principal:*

- *Understand the role of the superintendent. He's the
  head of the school district and the principal's boss.*
- *Use the right words to get in the door. Don't be
  confrontational—that won't end the bullying.*
- *Let the superintendent know that you talked with
  or met with the principal but that the bullying is
  still taking place.*

---

be enough to do this. It also serves as very important documentation of your actions and theirs in case you need to go further up the ladder—to the board of education or beyond.

HOW TO WRITE A LETTER TO THE SUPERINTENDENT

Remember Lisa, whose story was told in chapters three and four? The first time Lisa's mother approached the school, she didn't do it effectively. She and her husband went up the chain, meeting with Lisa's counselor, the principal, and the superintendent. But neither was prepared with a script; they did not have a copy of the school's antibullying policy; and both were unaware that if their pleas for help didn't produce fruit, they could take it up a notch by writing a firm letter that would force definitive intervention from the superintendent.

Nothing positive happened for Lisa until her mother sent a carefully worded letter to the superintendent. That letter had the right words and was the catalyst for the meeting that, in turn, ended Lisa's ordeal.

What follows are excerpts from the actual letter. After each excerpt, which is printed in *italics,* I'll explain why that language was important. Key considerations for your own letter appear in **bold type.**

> *Lisa has been the subject of harassment, intimidation, and bullying in school since January 2008.*

> When writing to the administration, **use language found in the board of education's policy.** In this case, the phrase *harassment, intimidation, and bullying* is taken directly from the policy, which Lisa's mother obtained before she wrote her letter.

Knowing exactly what the school board intended to address when it created the policy is a very effective way of communicating that you are an informed parent—and it holds the school to its own words.

We met on February 20, 2008, and presented an oral report to you regarding the situation, including information about what students were doing to Lisa. . . . According to your policy, this oral report is considered as an official reporting procedure.

Lisa's mother knows that the way she notified the school about her daughter's abuse "counts"—that is, **she established that a meeting took place and that she followed the school district's rules for reporting the bullying.** The words *an official reporting procedure* were taken directly from the board of education's policy.

We met with Lisa's teacher on March 12, 2008, and informed her of the harassment, intimidation, and bullying in school, including Lisa being pushed down the stairs and the fact that [Lisa] was fearful because of the presence in two of her classes of a male student who is the main perpetrator of the negative actions toward Lisa.

In your letter, **document every meeting and every promise.** This paragraph shows that Lisa's mother met with another school official. She captured the content of this meeting and documented it in her letter to the superintendent. (You might also want to send a thank-you note to whomever you meet with at the school, reiterating your concerns, what was discussed, and the plan that the school put forth to stop the bullying—just as you did with the principal. It will help you recall events later, if necessary.)

In addition, Lisa's counselor was called and made aware of these situations in school.

Name names. Make sure the superintendent knows about everyone with whom you have spoken about your child's situation. This passage documents that there was contact with, and a report to, yet another school official about Lisa's bullying.

The harassment, intimidation, and bullying continued in school, even after our meeting with you, [our] meeting with the teacher, and [our] call to the counselor.

Lisa's mother took extraordinary steps to inform the school about what was going on and asked for intervention to make it stop—with no positive result. **Has the school followed its own policies to end the bullying?** If you have notified the school and the bullying continues, it has not. In no uncertain terms, tell the school why.

Lisa, as a result of this harassment, intimidation, and bullying in school, feels insulted, demeaned, and fearful to the extent that in February of this school year, these issues caused her to manifest physical responses that necessitated medical treatment.

It is important to **document the pain and damage** that the bullying is having on your child. As we will see in chapter six, this lays the groundwork if you find it necessary to go beyond the school to other agencies or to file a lawsuit.

On May 21, 2008, we met with Lisa's teacher and counselor and asked, as a way of addressing the situation, if Lisa could not be in the same class next year as the male student and one of the girls who are the perpetrators of this harassment. At this meeting, the issues of ha-

rassment, intimidation, and bullying were again discussed, and it was mentioned that Lisa was fearful, scared, and intimidated by the male student. Also at this meeting, it was suggested that Lisa meet with two of the girls who have been harassing and intimidating her in order to have "closure." As you may know, we chose for Lisa to not attend such a meeting since she is the brunt of this inappropriate behavior and not the cause.

Lisa's mother documented what she communicated to the school: **it is the school's responsibility—not that of the victim—to address the situation.** When the school suggested that Lisa meet with her tormenters, I told her mother not to allow it. Moreover, from February to May—a three-month period—nothing was resolved; in fact, the situation worsened.

All we want is for Lisa to be safe in school. She does not feel safe because of the behavior of other students toward her. . . . At this time we are asking that you intervene in order to implement your policy regarding a resolution of the issue.

After laying out the relevant sections of the school's policy and documenting attempts on her own part to resolve the bullying, **Lisa's mother made her expectations clear.**

We are requesting that the male student and the female student who are the perpetrators of the harassment, intimidation, and bullying of Lisa be scheduled so that they are not in any of Lisa's classes next year. According to the school's policy, this is an acceptable and appropriate remedial measure.

Be sure that your expectations are in line with school policy. In this case, the policy specifically states that the superintendent can implement this procedure. The superintendent either ignored this provision in the policy or truly didn't know it was there.

We would like to meet with you, the principal, and Lisa's counselor as soon as possible in order to obtain your commitment to this remedial measure so that the harassment, intimidation, and bullying of Lisa will be eliminated and so that she will be able to fully benefit from her education.

Lisa's mother clearly asked the superintendent to implement school policy—in this case, a measure that gives him the authority to put the students in different classes, away from Lisa. This paragraph also established that **Lisa's parents wanted their daughter to benefit fully from her education.** This is an important statement that we will discuss in chapter six. Federal laws require that schools eliminate situations that may prevent a student from fully benefiting from her education. If a student is bullied and does not go to school for several days because she is afraid, that student is missing her educational opportunity— she is not fully benefiting from her education. That is the fault of the school.

Three days after the letter was sent, the superintendent's secretary called Lisa's mother to set up a meeting attended by the attorney for the board of education. The superintendent and the school district's attorney knew, after reading this letter, that these parents were well informed. The administration knew that these parents had read the school's antibullying policy and that the school was dragging its feet in resolving the situation. The school needed to act swiftly. The only shame was that it took three months, many desperate telephone calls, and my intervention for the bullying to stop.

In this case, the meeting produced results that brought a quick end to Lisa's problems. Once everyone involved understood that the district could be held legally liable for not following its own state-mandated policy to intervene decisively on Lisa's behalf, the district took quick action. It placed Lisa's bullies in different classes; identified, with her input, a person on the faculty for her to go to if the bullying continued; and provided more opportunity for her to see her counselor. With all the attention today on the harms that occur when schools do not act on their responsibility to snuff out a bullying situation immediately, it's difficult to imagine that a situation would progress beyond this stage. Unfortunately, though, it can happen.

If you find yourself in that situation, your next stop is the board of education. To do this knowledgeably, you will benefit from understanding how school districts are set up and what a board of education is responsible for doing.

In your letter to the superintendent, it is important to do the following:

- *Use language from the board of education's policy.*
- *Describe whom you met with and what was promised to you.*
- *Show how you followed district policy in making requests.*
- *Illustrate why the school has not followed through on its responsibility to act.*
- *Document the damage the bullying has done to your child.*
- *Make it clear that you expect your child to benefit fully from her education.*

PUBLIC SCHOOL SYSTEMS: A PRIMER

Who runs the public education systems in the United States? You do, to an extent. As a taxpaying citizen, you have the right to vote on their governance. The federal government delegates the responsibility for educating the nation's children to the states. States set educational standards and allow their implementation to take place at the local level. This is dramatically different from what exists in most parts of the world, where schools are centralized and under federal control, usually through a government ministry of education.

What this means is that in the United States, there are 50 different state education systems. Moreover, within each state, many differences exist among local school systems.

Local school boards are considered creatures of the state and were devised for the purpose of running a *school district,* or system of schools. There are fifteen thousand local school districts in the United States. Though school districts are the domain of municipalities, the federal government has always had some say in public education by establishing broad rights for children so that kids can learn in an atmosphere free of obstacles, such as discrimination or educational bias. But with each school district at liberty to set its own policies for meeting state and federal laws, you can imagine how much room there is for the interpretation—and sometimes misunderstanding—of what's expected of them. Even informed parents—like you—need help from time to time to sort it out, at least when it comes to navigating your child's right to learn in a safe environment.

Let's start by taking a closer look at local school districts. To help you understand how to work with a board of education, here's a quick civics lesson of sorts: what a school district is, how it is organized, and how it is run.

LOCAL SCHOOL DISTRICTS

Every public school in the United States is part of a local school district created by the state. The school district is more than a collection of schools in your area; it provides a way for you to have a say in how state and federal educational mandates should be carried out in your city or town. Because a school district's purpose is to carry out a state function (public education), its policies must be consistent with policies in the state's school code. The local school district, as an example, must develop curricula that meet the state's minimum educational standards for reading, math, and other subjects.

School districts vary in size, number of schools, and grade configuration. Some are large, comprising forty thousand students and as many as one hundred school buildings, while the smallest may be a single kindergarten-through-sixth-grade school in a single building with 42 students and four teachers. Some are organized into prekindergarten through grade five in one school building, grades six through eight in another, and grades nine through twelve in yet another. Whether your school district is small or large—and no matter what state you are in—your child's school is part of a district that develops policies based on state education laws, such as requirements for educating children with disabilities and, where bullying laws are in place, antibullying policies.

Whether your school district is small or large, and no matter what state you are in, your child's school is part of a district that must comply with state and federal education laws.

THE SCHOOL SUPERINTENDENT

The superintendent is the executive officer of the school district. One of her primary duties is to evaluate a principal's performance.

This review may be based on annual goals that involve things like the improvement of mathematics scores, the addition of a preschool program, or the development of procedures to monitor school dances. Another major function of the school superintendent is to gather and present data so that the board of education can make intelligent policy decisions. The superintendent provides vision, develops strategies for the growth or reduction of programs, and keeps school board members abreast of problems that may require changes in district policies.

The superintendent's powers are broad, and her many duties are wide-ranging. These typically include the following:

- serving as supervisor and organizer of personnel
- making recommendations about the employment, promotion, and dismissal of personnel
- ensuring compliance with directives of higher authority, such as those from state and federal departments of education
- preparing the school budget for board review and administering the adopted budget
- serving as leader of long-range planning
- developing and evaluating curricula and instructional programs
- determining the internal organization of the school district
- making recommendations about school-building and maintenance needs[4]

The most important thing for you to know is that the superintendent has the ultimate responsibility for implementing antibullying policies in each of the schools under her charge.

*The superintendent is the one who brings proposed policy
and curricular changes to the board of education.*

THE BOARD OF EDUCATION

If the superintendent is the executive officer of the school system, the board of education is the legislative policy-making body. Made up of elected or appointed members from the community, local school boards have significant decision-making responsibilities. One of these is the development of policies that protect your child from the harms of bullying. School boards make decisions on how schools in the district will implement antibullying programs, how they should train teachers in combating bullying, and how they will discipline students who are bullies.

In general, boards of education are beholden to two masters. They must conform to state guidelines to qualify for state aid. They also have to conform to federal guidelines in order to receive federal funding, such as money set aside for the education of children with disabilities.

It may come as some surprise to you that school boards consist of laypeople who are not usually experts in school affairs. In essence, the school board is the people's governance of the school district. One of the board's most important responsibilities, then, is to appoint a well-trained, competent superintendent of schools. The board also must see that the work of the school is properly performed by professional personnel who provide them with information about educational innovation, programs, statistics about dropout rates, the percentage of students meeting the state education standards, and the hiring of staff, to name a few. As laypeople, board members often delegate many of their own legal powers to the superintendent and his staff.

The job of running a school is much like running a business. School board members must demonstrate good business practices. Board members must be fair and mindful of the law when dealing with students, teachers, administrators, parents, and other community residents. They go to an annual state convention to learn about budgeting, special education, and other matters so that they can perform their duties well. As elected officials, board members are public servants—they represent the community and are expected to govern the school system through the approval of a superintendent's policies without encroaching on the authority of the superintendent.

If that sounds like a school board member has a lot of power, she does—but in a limited way. If you are a police officer, you know the drill: even when you are off duty, you are "on" because neighbors and others know what you do—and because you have the authority to uphold the law even when you are off the clock. The members of the board of education, however, have no power except during a board meeting and only while acting as a collective group.[5] This is an important point to understand. If your neighbor is on the school board, you might think he can change school policy, punish bullies, or reprimand the principal if you bring it up with him at your next backyard barbecue. This is not the case. He has power *only* when the school board convenes at an official board meeting.

In addition, there is a formal procedure that has to be followed if you want the board to hear your concerns. Your issue has to be placed on the school board meeting agenda, or you can bring it up at points during the meeting when the public can address the board or when board members can consider any other business not on the agenda. The board will discuss your issue, and if it warrants a possible change of school policy, then the entire board must vote—not whether to change the policy, but whether to consider doing so.

If the board agrees to consider a change, the board will review the current policy, conduct studies if necessary under the direction of the superintendent, and place the policy change or new policy development on a future board agenda. When the proposed change comes up at a future board meeting, there is a discussion and then a vote.

> *The members of the board of education have the power to consider or make changes to district policies only during official school board meetings.*

ADDRESSING THE BOARD OF EDUCATION

Outside, it was a chilly early May night in northeastern Indiana. But inside, where the Smith-Green Community Board of School Trustees was meeting, the room was hot and stuffy as tempers neared a boiling point.

Parents packed the administrative center to tell the school board their concerns about children being bullied at the local high school. Six parents took their turns at the microphone. One told the board that he did not want to make his complaints at a public meeting but that the school administration's inaction had forced his hand. Another said that she had repeatedly told teachers and administrators about her child being bullied, but nothing had been done about it.[6]

If after talking with your child's teachers, the principal, and the superintendent your child is still being bullied by the kids in her class, the next step is to address your local board of education. This may seem to be a long and drawn-out process—but like other bureaucracies, this is the way our education system works. If this takes too long and your child is in danger, there are options you can take outside the school district and the structure of the educational enterprise. We will talk about those in chapter six.

Your board of education should publish information about how you can notify them about your concern. To find out, go to your school district's website and search for "board of education meetings" or "how to address the board."

Here's what the board of education for a relatively small school district in Michigan published:

MEET THE BOARD OF EDUCATION AND SUPERINTENDENT

The Board of Education welcomes you to attend its meetings. All meetings are open to the public so that citizens may have the benefit of hearing Board deliberations. All formal action by the Board of Education takes place during the public meetings. Executive (closed) sessions may be held to discuss personnel matters, the purchase or sale of property for competitive bidding, disputes involving court action, negotiations with employees, and certain school security matters.

We encourage you to express your views on subjects related to our schools. Comments are welcome during the times designated on each regular Board agenda. A copy of the meeting agenda is available on an information counter near the entrance to the meeting room.

The Board of Education meets the second and fourth Tuesday of each month except July, August, and December. All regular meeting dates are published in the *Reporter* newspaper. Any changes and special meetings are posted in the Board of Education office.

HOW TO ADDRESS THE BOARD OF EDUCATION

The public may address the Board at their regular meetings during the two times indicated on the agenda using the following procedures:

- Remarks by individuals are limited to three minutes. Individuals should state name, address, and organization represented. During this time, the Board listens to comments from the public but does not engage in dialogue or render decisions.

- If a large group plans to attend, notification should be made to the school prior to the meeting to assure seating for the group. They are requested to select up to five representatives to speak on their behalf for a total of not more than 15 minutes.

- Individuals addressing the Board shall abide by the rules of common courtesy. The meeting cannot be used to make personal attacks against a Board member or district employee which are totally unrelated to the manner in which the Board member or employee performs his duties.

- An individual wishing to address the Board of Education and needing more than the three minutes should make his/her request to the Superintendent at least seven days before the regular meeting so that an appropriate length of time (no more than 15 minutes) may be indicated on the agenda.

IF YOU HAVE SPECIAL CONCERNS

Often individual concerns can be handled if you begin at the source and follow proper channels before approaching members of the Board of Education. If your concern relates to procedures in the classroom, begin with the teacher and/or principal. Problems related to other services can best be dealt with by those department heads.

The assistant superintendents and superintendent can provide additional help.

Finally, if these procedures do not resolve your concern or question, the Board of Education may be contacted. For information on this procedure, contact the Superintendent's office.[7]

To borrow from an old expression, if you've seen one school district, you've seen one school district. As you will see from the next example, the specifics of how you can bring a concern to the board differ from district to district—so it's best to check your district's protocol before you begin. Here's how the board of education in a larger school district in Ohio wants parents to do business with it:

MAKING A PRESENTATION TO THE BOARD

To speak before the Board, please contact the [district]. You will be asked to identify yourself, any organization you represent, and the topic you wish to speak about. At the meeting, you may want to provide 15 copies of any material for distribution. Your presentation should be no longer than 3 minutes.

PUBLIC PARTICIPATION AT BOARD MEETINGS

The Board desires citizens of the district to attend its sessions so that they may become better acquainted with the public schools and so that the Board may hear the ideas and wishes of the public.

To permit citizens to be heard and at the same time conduct its meetings efficiently, the Board will hear from the public only at times scheduled for such comments and presentations on the meeting agenda.

At each meeting, the agenda will set aside time when spokespersons for school-related organizations may comment or make presentations. Time also will be scheduled for presentations/comments by spokespersons for nonschool-related groups and individuals. Comments and presentations by school-related and nonschool-related spokespersons will be limited to three minutes per person and fifteen minutes per topic, except as additional time is granted. The Board President has the discretion to modify the time limits outlined in the prior sentence. The Board President may, if requested by the public, schedule a special meeting for the purpose of hearing public comment on a specific topic.

The Board requires that an individual or community group desiring to make a presentation on a particular topic submit a request in writing, by fax, or by a phone call, to the school district Treasurer/designee no later than noon the day of the meeting. This request should include each speaker's complete name; the full address of each speaker; the topic that will be addressed by each speaker; and when possible, one written copy of the statement each speaker is to make before the Board.

When addressing the Board, the speaker will direct questions to the President of the Board. The Board President, or a Board Member, may ask a speaker questions in order to clarify the discussion. No speaker will use employees' names or present complaints against individual employees in a public meeting. In addition, discussion of matters currently under legal review will not be permitted.

The President of the Board may terminate the comments of any speaker whose remarks are abusive, defamatory, or designed to disrupt the meeting.[8]

Boards of education function differently when it comes to addressing your issues. It's important for you to find out how your board will address your issue of bullying.

FEDERAL PROTECTIONS

If by now you are thinking, "The teacher, principal, and superintendent didn't address my child's situation—why would the board of education be any different?" then consider this: federal funding may be at stake, especially if your child's civil rights are being violated. That's why the public school system has an interest in listening to you.

The U.S. Office for Civil Rights (OCR) enforces federal civil rights laws that prohibit discrimination on the basis of race, color, national origin, sex, disability, and age in programs or activities that receive funding from the Department of Education. Your local school district receives federal financial assistance for such things as its lunch program, special-education programs and services, and other remedial education services for low-functioning students. These civil rights laws extend to all state education agencies, elementary and secondary school systems, colleges and universities, vocational schools, proprietary schools, vocational rehabilitation agencies, libraries, and museums that receive federal financial assistance from the Department of Education.

Keep in mind that if your child is in a private school, you do not have the option to rely upon these laws because private schools do not receive federal financial assistance. Indeed, many private schools are formed so that the school does not have to comply with federal education requirements. This places the parent of a private school student at a disadvantage. Remember that, unlike a public school, a private school does not have to accept your child's enrollment. If the private school doesn't like your child or your complaints about bullying, the headmaster can show you the door. (In chapter six, I'll talk about what legal recourse you have if this happens.)

Anyone who believes that an educational institution that receives federal financial assistance has discriminated against someone on the basis of race, color, national origin, sex, disability, or age may file a complaint. The person who files the complaint does not need to be a victim of the discrimination and may file a complaint on behalf of another person or group.

TYPES OF HARASSMENT: IN DEPTH

DISABILITY HARASSMENT

Students with disabilities all too often become the brunt of abusive jokes, crude name-calling, threats, and bullying—and even sexual and physical assault by teachers and other students. In my opinion, this type of bullying is the worst type. This type of disregard for the differences among us represents, in my view, the most callous form of inhumanity there is. Earlier, I introduced you to two of my grandchildren—Silas, aka "the Panda," and Victoria, my granddaughter with Down syndrome. The Panda was bullied because he was different. He was different because of his disability. When the school knows about this type of bullying and does not act to stop it, it is discriminating against a student with a disability. When Victoria was put into the "time-out" room— the six-by-six-foot cinder-block closet—by her teacher simply because the teacher became frustrated with her behavior, that too was disability harassment because the teacher failed to take into consideration the fact that Victoria was not able to express her thoughts verbally.

The Office of Special Education and Rehabilitative Services is an agency within the U.S. Department of Education. This agency enforces a school district's responsibilities under special-education laws. These laws, commonly called "Section 504," "IDEA," and "Title II,"[9] ensure that eligible students with disabilities receive a free appropriate public education. If your child endures disability harassment, he may be denied a free appropriate public education. Parents may initiate administrative due process procedures under Section 504, IDEA, or Title II.

Just what is disability harassment? Under Section 504 and Title II, disability harassment is intimidation, abusive behavior, or bullying toward a student that is based on that student's disability and that creates a hostile environment and interferes with that student's chance to get an education or participate in school programs. Bullying and harassment can include name-calling; graphic and written statements; or conduct that is physically threatening, harmful, or humiliating.

When bullying and harassment are so severe, persistent, or pervasive that they create a "hostile environment," it can violate a student's rights under Section 504 and Title II. By the time Daryl, the student council president whom you met in chapter one, had spun Taya's wheelchair into a wall, he had already terrorized her to the point where she had repeated nightmares about him coming after her with a gun. A hostile environment may exist even if there are no tangible effects on the student. Here are some examples of bullying that could create a hostile environment:

- Several students continually remark out loud during class that a student with dyslexia is "retarded" and does not belong in the class; as a result, the bullied student has difficulty doing work in class and her grades go down.
- A student repeatedly places classroom furniture or other objects in the path of a classmate who uses a wheelchair, impeding her ability to enter the classroom.
- A teacher subjects a student to inappropriate physical restraint because of conduct related to his disability, with the result that the student tries to stay home from school.[10]
- A school administrator repeatedly denies a student with a disability access to lunch, field trips, assemblies, or extracurricular activities as punishment for classroom absences for receiving medical or other services related to the student's disability.

- Students continually taunt or belittle a student with mental retardation by mocking and intimidating him so that he does not participate in class.

In these cases—or in any whereby disability-related bullying limits or denies a student's ability to participate in school activities—the school must respond effectively. When the school learns that disability harassment may have occurred, the school must investigate promptly and respond appropriately. When the school does not respond appropriately, the bullying will continue.

There is a caveat to filing a federal discrimination case, and it's important to know: you won't be able to jump right to the feds if you think your child's continued bullying constitutes a civil rights violation. This is when you need to follow the steps in this book: find out the facts from your child; contact the teacher and principal; and if the bullying doesn't stop, move on to the superintendent and the board of education. *These steps must be followed first before the Office for Civil Rights (OCR) will investigate a complaint.*

Harassing conduct also may violate state and local civil rights, child abuse, or criminal laws. Some of these laws may require public schools to contact or coordinate with state or local agencies or police when it comes to disability harassment. If a school does not follow appropriate procedures under these laws, it can find itself in legal trouble—another reason the board of education has an interest in listening to you. I will cover more about this in chapter six.

RACIAL AND ETHNIC HARASSMENT

Remember Darek from chapter four? He was bullied by the principal, who treated him differently than a group of other kids who were involved in the same activity. He was treated differently—and discriminated against—because of his Middle Eastern heritage. His classmates received a three-day suspension, but Darek got a four-day suspension. The extra day of suspension allowed the school to recommend that he be transferred involuntarily to a different school. It was the school's way of trying to get rid of him.

About a week after the events of September 11, 2001, then-secretary of education Rod Paige issued a letter reminding schools of the prohibition against racial or ethnic harassment and bullying. In particular, it focused on harassment against Muslim and Arab students. In the days and weeks after the attacks on the World Trade Center and the Pentagon, there were reports of harassment and violence directed at students perceived to be of Middle Eastern origin. Parents expressed fear about the safety of their children at school.

In his letter, Paige said, "We are all committed to making sure children across America can attend school in a safe and secure environment free from physical threats and discrimination. School officials, working closely with students, parents, and community groups, play a critical role in ensuring that race-based harassment and violence have no place in our schools."[11] Paige's message underscored the idea that if harassment and bullying are left unchecked, they can jeopardize students' ability to learn, undermine their physical and emotional well-being, provoke retaliatory violence, and exacerbate community conflicts.

You can file a complaint with the OCR office if you believe that your child has been the victim of bullying based on race or ethnicity. Again, OCR will require that you work through your local school district before filing a federal complaint.

A school's federal funding may be at stake, especially if your child's civil rights are violated. That's why the public school system has an interest in listening to you.

HOW DO YOU FILE A COMPLAINT?

If you file a complaint with the OCR, you must file within 60 days after the last act of the school district's grievance process. In other words, you have 60 days after you have (a) sent a letter to the board of education complaining about your child's disability or ethnic harassment and (b) received an unsatisfactory solution from the board to file a complaint with the OCR.

You can mail, fax, or email your complaint or use the OCR's online complaint form at http://www2.ed.gov/about/offices/list/ocr/complaintintro.html.

Your correspondence must include the following:

- your name; address; and if possible, a telephone number where you can be reached during business hours
- information about your child, such as your child's name, grade, and age
- the name and location of your child's school
- a description of the alleged discriminatory act; be sure to include enough detail so that the OCR understands what occurred and when, as well as the basis for your complaint (e.g., was the alleged discrimination based on race, color, national origin, sex, or disability?)

You will hear back from the OCR about your complaint. The OCR will determine whether the complaint merits an investigation. The school will receive a copy of your complaint, so it will be on notice that you have filed with the OCR.[12]

GOING BEYOND THE EDUCATIONAL SYSTEM

If you followed the school's procedures for bringing your concern to the board of education, if you did not get a satisfactory resolution, and if the OCR either declines to investigate or does investigate and determines your claim is without merit, is there more you can do? Yes. That's the topic of chapter six.

You might also find yourself in a situation in which you can't wait for the bureaucracy and need to take immediate action outside of contacting the teacher, principal, superintendent, or the board of education. This is an emergency that is caused when your son is punched in the face and loses three teeth or when your daughter is stalked and taunted by a group of kids, making her fear for her life. In these and other situations, it is necessary to go to local law enforcement authorities immediately. I will cover how to do that in the next chapter.

CHAPTER SIX

THE LEGAL FACE OF BULLYING

CRIMINAL AND CIVIL LAWS

KEYCEPT: School bullying is terrible and cruel. But is it a crime? Some states have criminal laws against harassment and stalking. Prosecutors can rely on both when filing criminal charges against school bullies. As a parent, you can't bring criminal charges against individuals for harassment, stalking, or other persecution against your child. Only a prosecutor can do this if the law provides for it. You can, however, invoke civil laws when you believe your child has been physically or emotionally harmed because the school ignored bullying and allowed it to fester.

In this chapter, you will learn when it's time to use the legal system and how to do so. You will learn how to report bullying to local law enforcement and how criminal laws address school bullying. You will also learn about lawsuits—and when it might be necessary to file a lawsuit against the board of education. You will learn what to look for in a lawyer and what to talk about. You will also learn how an attorney evaluates whether a lawsuit has merit, as well as what to expect when a lawsuit is filed.

Jennifer Adkins's desperate attempt to reach her son holds a tragic end. Fourteen-year-old Christopher Jones had been having difficulties with neighborhood bullies, one of whom had recently threatened to stab him in the school cafeteria. After that moment, Adkins made it a practice to text or call Chris every half hour to make sure he was safe.

This time, Chris was not answering his cell phone.

Standing just blocks from her suburban Maryland home, Adkins heard sirens. On the very street Chris lived, teenage gang members had surrounded the boy on his bicycle and viciously punched him over and over as he tried to pedal home. He died at the scene when his bicycle went down and his head hit the pavement—even as his phone kept buzzing in his pocket.

When his life was threatened in the spring of 2009, Chris was a ninth grader at Arundel High School. According to the family's attorney, Adkins repeatedly called Tanja Wheeler, an assistant principal, to discuss the incident. When the two finally met, Wheeler suggested that Chris be transferred to South River High School, and she promised to notify the police and take other steps to protect Chris.

The transfer took place, but that was all. A month later, Chris was dead.

The family filed lawsuits totaling $10 million against the Anne Arundel County Board of Education, the two youths who were convicted of manslaughter in Chris's death, and the parents of the four other teens who were accused of egging on the attackers. The lawsuit seeks $200,000 from the school system, the maximum allowed under that state's law. (It should be noted here that some state laws limit the amount of money that can be recovered from a public entity such as a public school. You need to discuss this with an attorney. Of course, it's not about getting money—it's about the safety of kids and holding schools responsible to protect them. But this is how the legal system works. As a parent, you have a right to sue the school system if you believe that it has breeched its duty to protect your child, and this violation caused injury to your child. Once you go to a lawyer, it takes on a life of its own.) The suit alleges that Wheeler "failed to take any action to fulfill" her promise to safeguard Chris.[1]

As well-meaning as your principal may seem to be when talking with you about the bullying of your child, you can't always count on her to take decisive action. A school district's approach to bully prevention may seem comprehensive—but if it's not enforced, your child can still be harmed. By reading this far, you have learned how to find out what's going on with your child; how to document that information; how to discuss it with the teacher, principal, superintendent, and the board of education; and—if necessary—how to communicate discrimination against your child to federal authorities. At this point, if the bullying continues and you have gotten nowhere, you have legal options.

In this chapter, you'll learn what these options are and when to take them. Some situations warrant immediate action. Others require that you first apply what you've learned in the previous chapters. You'll read many real-life stories about bullying that were brought to court through either the criminal justice system or the civil system. Compare these situations to your own to begin to make decisions about whether to pursue either of these choices or both.

WHEN YOUR HAND IS FORCED

If your son was beaten up in school as a culmination of weeks of bullying, you should call the police, file a complaint, and contact an attorney. If you have effectively communicated with the school and the bullies still continue to harass your daughter, you should contact an attorney.

In South Hadley, Massachusetts, where Phoebe Prince was bullied before she hanged herself, the prosecutor arrested six students at South Hadley High School and charged them with crimes associated with her death. This is an example of the application of *criminal law*, or *penal law*, to the result of bullying. A *civil lawsuit* against a school for neglecting its duty to enforce its antibullying policy—which, in turn, leads to harm (in this example, Phoebe's suicide)—is also an option. (As of this writing, Phoebe's mother and the school reached an undisclosed monetary settlement and the case did not proceed to a civil trial.)

Parents shouldn't have to sue to protect their children from bullies at school, and their children should never have to live in fear of going to school. But sometimes—when nothing else you tried prevented your child from being harmed—suing the school has to be done. It certainly causes the school to sit up and take notice.

With the intense media focus on the suicides of children who were bullied and the awarding of damages to students who were bullied by classmates, it's likely that we will see even more litigation against school districts than we already have. If parents don't learn how to communicate effectively with the school so that schools are held accountable to antibullying laws and their own antibullying policies, the pace of litigation will continue to escalate.

But for better or worse? That depends on how you look at it.

Pursuing justice through the legal system is stressful for all involved—the child, the family, and the community. It's generally best if you try to work with the school first. Working to develop a positive relationship with the school will, in the end, strengthen community, as parents and schools work together for the benefit of kids.

Legal action changes the dynamic—from one that is cooperative to one that is adversarial—and the damage can be irreversible. It weakens community.

That said, there are some conditions under which legal action is important to pursue. Legal action certainly raises attention to the issue of bullying and causes schools to pay attention to areas where they might be lacking. For example, if your child was bullied and you notified the school about it, yet she can't even enter the science room because the bullies are there, her grades go down, you talk to the principal again and nothing changes, and your child is now seeing a psychologist because of her school phobia, it's time to talk with an attorney. The school is forcing your hand. You have tried the best you can. You developed a script, called the principal, and gave her two weeks to make good on her promises. When it didn't happen and you can't get satisfaction as you move up the chain of command, you have to protect your child. Sometimes, the only way to do that is by filing a lawsuit or going to the police.

Try to work with the school first. If the bullying continues or if your child is physically or emotionally harmed, your best option for protecting your child is to go to the police or talk with an attorney about a civil lawsuit.

THE CRIMINAL SIDE OF BULLYING

Bullying is hurtful. But is *bullying* a crime? It can be, but not by that name.

Most states have antibullying laws, but these laws do not codify bullying as a crime. Instead, they direct schools to develop antibullying policies. The scope of bullying is so broad that defining it for the purpose of criminalizing it is difficult to do. As a result, bullying is typically prosecuted under existing laws that govern behavior.

In California, for instance, the Education Code describes bullying with regard to suspending or expelling a student, but bullying is not listed as a specific crime in the California Penal Code. Instead, alleged acts of bullying must fit the definition of an existing crime—such as criminal threats, assault, battery, sexual battery, hate crimes, or harassing electronic communication—for a prosecution to take place.

The types of bullying that could result in a prosecution include the following:

- physical or sexual assault or threatened assault
- deliberate damage to property
- harassing phone calls
- stalking

When Phoebe Prince killed herself, allegedly because of the torment she endured at South Hadley High School, the Massachusetts prosecutor filed felony charges against six students. The prosecutor applied the state's criminal harassment and criminal stalking laws to the actions of the students. This case adds to the landscape of responses to bullying: now, bullies may face jail time. Nothing will get kids to sit up and take notice more than when one of their peers ends up in jail.

Interestingly, Phoebe's father said that it never should have come to this. In interviews with the *Boston Globe* and *Irish Central.com* seven months after Phoebe's suicide, Jeremy Prince, who lives in Ireland, said that his daughter probably felt like she was in a no-win situation. Phoebe didn't tell her mother how bad the bullying had become in the days leading up to her death, he said, most likely out of fear that it would have made the bullying worse. If Phoebe's mother had understood the depth of her daughter's anguish in those final days, he said, she would have marched right into the school—and the administrators would have done nothing substantive about it. "The adults at the high school responded to this like administrators, not educators. Administrators minimize everything. They want as little hassle as possible. An educator would be setting an example," he said. "This is what drove her to suicide."[2]

SOMETIMES, LAWMAKERS DO LISTEN

In response to Phoebe's death, Massachusetts passed a comprehensive antibullying law. Even this law does not criminalize bullying per se. It does, however, describe how bullying that commonly occurs at schools can be defined as such crimes as stalking or criminal harassment. Under the Massachusetts law, if an incident is deemed to be potential criminal activity, the principal is required to notify law enforcement officials.

Through the diligence of parents and advocacy organizations that clamored for better protection for their children, the law that finally emerged from Massachusetts was among the nation's strongest. It was hailed by Bully Police USA as "a good law"—one of the nation's best that earned its highest grade, A++.[3] Sometimes, lawmakers do listen.

They listened in New Hampshire, too, where adults and students lobbied for stricter standards to protect children after stories like that of Anastasia Holt made the news.

"They call me fat, call me ugly," said Anastasia, then 17. Kids told her that no one could ever love her because she's disgusting. It got so bad for her, she said, that she would avoid school. "I would go to the nurse's office on a daily basis, saying I was too sick to be at school," she said.[4]

Such stories of relentless harassment prompted enhancements to New Hampshire's antibullying law, the outcome being a tougher approach to a persistent problem. The law, which passed in 2010 and raised New Hampshire's Bully Police USA grade from C to A++, broadens definitions of what constitutes bullying and adds cyberbullying to that list. It forces educators to watch what kids are saying or doing and to pay more attention to students' changes in mood.

Under New Hampshire law, all school staff members have to have annual training on how to recognize bullying or cyberbullying and how it should be reported. Each school district must now write a policy on how to deal with bullying and how teachers and the school can protect accusers. Unlike before, a single incident—instead of a series of events—can now be considered bullying. The school must also notify parents of bullying incidences within two days. Under the new law, bullying can include an incident off of school property if it interferes with a child's educational opportunities.

The New Hampshire law breaks new ground in that if a bullying situation is brought to school and creates a hostile environment, the school has a responsibility to get involved. That means that a school's protection covers some home activities, such as online activity or texting. It can also include what happens at a bus stop. Keep in mind that this is relevant in New Hampshire. It's important to check your own state's law to see if it covers these areas as extensively.

REWIRING THE TEEN BRAIN?

Middle school—that's the time to get to them. Children in middle school are at an age when they are developing friendships based on common interests rather than convenience, as they did when they were younger. It's when kids start to become more socially conscious, it's when their bodies start to change, and it's when they start to experience the injustice of bullying in a big way—as a victim, as a bully, or as an eyewitness.

Up the Potomac from Washington, D.C., Urbana Middle School has done more than hold just the occasional antibullying assembly. It actively tries to make antibullying part of the school culture. Don't bully, don't cheer the bullies on, don't just stand by and watch, and tell an adult when you see bullying happen—these themes are woven into the school's curriculum. Kids learn about the consequences of their actions. Parents are enlisted in the effort so that they give their children messages that are consistent with the things the kids learn at school. And the kids seem receptive to the effort.[5]

In Lawrence, Massachusetts, Frost Middle School teaches fifth graders lessons on bullying, empathy, and kindness during physical education, art, and English classes. Posters hung around the school encourage kids to "take a stand. Stop bullying now." Lawrence police visit the school to help kids understand what they can do when they are being bullied. When the fifth graders move on to sixth grade, they become mentors to the new fifth graders. Kids there say they like the difference in the atmosphere.[6]

Remember from chapter three that the teenage brain is not fully formed and that, as a result, teenagers are impulsive and don't usually think of the consequences of their actions. It's as if the Urbana and Frost middle schools are tackling this proactively—getting kids not only to recognize bullying when they see it, but to understand how it affects others. By making this part of children's culture while they are young, perhaps schools can help rewire kids' brains before many kids become less malleable as teenagers.

The schools' proactive approach isn't necessarily all about good citizenship, though. In part, the schools are responding to tough laws in their states that clamp down on bullying. Urbana Middle School principal Frank Vetter told National Public Radio that telling kids to stay out of fights is the law. Maryland requires schools to report all instances of bullying to the state. And in Lawrence, awareness of bullying is undoubtedly sky high because of what happened to Phoebe Prince just one hundred miles away and because of the stringent antibullying law Massachusetts enacted in tow.

Can teaching kids empathy work? In Saugatuck, Michigan, a comprehensive antibullying program in middle and high schools reported reduced incidences of bullying by about 35 percent. At Saugatuck High School, the results were particularly evident, with reported incidences in the 2009–2010 school year declining 60 percent from the previous year.[7]

Success stories like these are rarely reported. The media like sensationalism, of course, and the story of a child hanging herself sells more papers than a story about two kids shaking hands. Other stories of successful intervention take place below the media radar, handled by parents or schools—or between attorneys if a lawsuit is filed—and are settled long before a case gets to court. But as states enact new or tougher laws to keep schools on their toes, there is hope that schools' efforts will yield more success stories. As a parent, you can and should work with schools to make that happen.

One area in which a school's legal responsibility remains murky is cyberbullying. When is a school expected to address a problem that takes place off campus? Jill Eckel, principal at Sussex County Charter School for Technology—a middle school in Sparta, New Jersey—has heard from parents that it's not her business to monitor the online activities of her students. So when she heard about a student's MySpace page that was promoting an upcoming off-campus fight involving students at her school, those parents' warnings played back in her head. "I sat for a long time, thinking, 'Is it my responsibility to call the parents?'" she told a reporter.[8]

But she thought about the kids, too—and about the violence, the potential for injury and police involvement, and the culture of the school. Finally, she decided to call a parent she trusted, who in turn contacted the parents of several of the students involved. The incident was averted.

I'll talk more about schools' evolving legal responsibilities with respect to cyberbullying in chapter seven.

States are quickly passing new or tougher antibullying laws. Your involvement with the school can help to determine the success of these initiatives at the local level.

NAVIGATING THE LAW

There have been numerous situations in which charges have been brought against students for their role in bullying. One of the difficulties with criminalizing bullying, though, is the standard that is used. Does the state base the charges on the nature of the bullying itself or on the response of the victim? In other words, does the state bring charges, for instance, under the state's criminal stalking law against a student who follows and relentlessly harasses another? Or does the state charge the student with criminal harassment only when the bullied student becomes sufficiently fearful for her life?

There are times when a clear-cut case of bullying just doesn't fit neatly with existing law.

A 14-year-old boy on the Milford (Ohio) High School freshman basketball team experienced humiliation that nobody should have to endure. A teammate rubbed his genitals in the victim's face while others held him down, according to court filings. At times, when the boy ran up to the basket to take a shot, the bully would push him to the floor, stand over him, and say, "Just quit." The victim's parents filed suit against the school and the coach, claiming that the boy had been victimized under the state's hazing statute.

The judge dismissed the case. Why?

"The type of bullying present in this case, which was ostensibly done in order to induce [the victim] and perhaps certain other basketball players to quit the team . . . is an entirely different type of behavior which is separate and apart from hazing," wrote Common Pleas Court Judge Jerry McBride. He encouraged the legislature to enact a new law to deal with this type of bullying. The judge also dismissed claims of negligent supervision against the coach. Ohio law at the time granted the school and its personnel immunity in a case like this.[9]

In some situations, it's just not the right time or place to invoke the law.

Two families in South Hadley, Massachusetts, filed civil harassment complaints—not against the school, but against each other. A *civil harassment complaint* is not a *civil lawsuit*. It is a complaint filed with law enforcement claiming that your civil rights were criminally violated by another person.

According to published reports, Beth Coushaine's 12-year-old son was bullied by a bigger boy for a year. The 13-year-old bully sat on Beth's son and banged his head on lockers until it reached a point where the younger boy was afraid to go to school.

Coushaine said that she repeatedly asked officials at Michael E. Smith Middle School to intervene but got no satisfaction. Principal Erika A. Faginski-Stark and Assistant Principal Vincent Napoli advised her instead to go to the police, which Coushaine did—filing both criminal and civil complaints against the 13-year-old boy. The family of the accused boy filed a cross-complaint against Coushaine's child. Eventually, both sides dropped their civil complaints, and the 13-year-old was barred from being in the same classroom as Coushaine's son and from coming within a certain distance of him on school grounds.[10]

No parent wants to become embroiled in this kind of wrangle with another family. If Coushaine had known how to communicate effectively with the principal and assistant principal in the middle school, and if the school had dealt accordingly with the bullying situation, these families probably could have avoided much heartache and stress, not to mention the legal expense. I can understand the frustration that Coushaine felt when school officials glibly told her to go to the police. In essence, the school failed to follow through on its responsibility to protect her son from bullying. So, she went to the police and things got even more complicated when she sought a criminal complaint. This is a situation in which warring kids are reinforced by parents who themselves might become bullies. These things tend to take on a life of their own, with no way out without losing face.

My advice is to use the steps in the previous chapters before getting embroiled in the criminal or legal system. Sometimes you have to go the legal route, but in the case of these South Hadley parents, I don't believe this was one of those times. That is a personal choice, however—one that you can weigh against factors like the community response, the pain your child is suffering, the severity of a single incident or the magnitude of multiple incidents, and the response of the school.

In contrast to Michael E. Smith Middle School, Salem High School in New Hampshire handled a bullying situation as it should have and appropriately involved the authorities.

A 16-year-old girl wound up in a psychiatric hospital for a week as a result of being picked on in class about her sports interests, the way she looked, and her sexual orientation. She sent her mother a text message from the classroom to say that she couldn't take the bullying anymore and wanted to hurt herself. Her mother notified the school, which contacted the police. Moving swiftly, the school removed the girl from her classroom. Five students were charged with criminal harassment.

School officials—as they should have—suspended the five students for varying lengths of time, depending on the nature of their involvement. In response to the incident, the school also reviewed its bullying policy with staff and held assemblies for students about the consequences of bullying. Under the circumstances, the school's actions were appropriate. It acted quickly to investigate and to apply the school's student discipline code. What this school did—something most others don't do—was to notify the police. This school had a school resource officer on staff—a police officer trained to work with school kids—who had a direct link to the police department.[11]

Schools might notify the police depending on the agreements they have with local police departments and prosecutors' offices, and whether the local police departments assign school resource officers to the schools.

If you have a question as to whether the bully of your child violated criminal law, contact the police or the prosecutor's office and find out. Then make the decision as to whether you want to pursue a report that might lead to criminal charges against the bully.

One of the difficulties with criminalizing bullying is the standard that is used to base a prosecution. There are times when a clear-cut case of bullying just doesn't fit neatly with existing law.

WHEN IT'S TIME TO TALK WITH A LAWYER

As I have said, you can't always count on the school to do the right thing. Not all schools will act as decisively as Salem High School did in the previous case. Take, for instance, Clarks Summit Elementary School's response to allegations against a special-education teacher who was confronted by teacher aides after she allegedly slapped a young girl on the face and told her mother that the child's swollen lip resulted from a fall.

The teacher aides reported the special-education teacher to her supervisor, but they were reprimanded by the principal of the northeastern Pennsylvania school for "breaking a silent code," according to court documents. The teacher, Susan Wzorek, and her superiors ultimately found themselves on the wrong end of a lawsuit alleging that she abused seven autistic children and that her superiors covered it up. The suit claimed that Wzorek pulled students' hair, stomped on their feet, and strapped them to chairs with duct tape and bungee cords. The students, who could communicate only with picture cards, were unable to complain verbally about their ordeal.

Wzorek wound up facing both criminal and civil penalties—six weeks in prison after pleading no contest to reckless endangerment, and a $5 million settlement of a federal lawsuit, which also named the school district and Wzorek's superiors.[12]

When is it time to talk with a lawyer about a lawsuit? When you have done all that you can with the school to prevent your child from harm and yet harm is done, you should talk with a lawyer who has expertise in education law. This may not always be easy to find; most lawyers do not have training in education law and have little experience in the realm of schools and education matters. Check with your state's bar association for a listing of lawyers who list themselves as having such experience.

Some lawyers experienced in accidents and wrongful-death matters sometimes venture into the area of school litigation. When a good lawyer lacking specific expertise in education law feels that there is merit to a case, she will contact a litigation consultant with education, training, and personal and professional experience in education administration. In other words, she will seek out an expert witness—someone who will offer an opinion as to whether a school acted reasonably, given what it knew was happening.

TYPICAL PROGRESSION OF A LAWSUIT

A federal jury in Detroit awarded $800,000 to a boy who had been bullied by classmates for years until he was finally sexually assaulted. In *David Patterson and Dena Patterson v. Hudson Area Schools and Kathy Malnar,* the Pattersons accused the school district of violating a federal ban on sex discrimination in schools called Title IX.[13] The suit alleged that the school district knew about the bullying but did not do enough to stop it.

At issue were two questions: Did the school district make sufficient efforts to stop the harassment? And did the bullying continue? In this case, the court held that although the school had implemented several proactive programs to combat bullying, the school remained "deliberately indifferent" toward the Pattersons' son—one of the required elements to establish a violation of Title IX. When the boy reached the ninth grade and his harassment intensified, "Hudson's only response was to employ the same type of verbal reprimands that it had used unsuccessfully in response to the sixth- and seventh-grade harassment," according to the ruling by the Sixth Circuit Court of Appeals. These steps, the court ruled, "were clearly unreasonable in light of the known circumstances."[14]

As an expert in education administration, school safety, and education law, I review documents associated with school-related lawsuits and render an opinion as to whether the school acted reasonably under the circumstances. These circumstances include what the school knew about the bullying and whether its response based on what it knew met the standard of professional practice in education administration and student supervision. Simply put, did the school act appropriately to protect your child?

In the Michigan case just described, the federal court said no— the school's actions were not reasonable under the circumstances. The same holds true for your child's school if it repeatedly uses the same unsuccessful approach with the bully and the bullying continues or intensifies. In such a situation, your child's school is not acting reasonably if it knows what is happening to him.

Let's say, on the other hand, that your child's school takes multiple approaches to end the bullying: among perhaps other measures, it conducts an investigation, it goes into the classroom and reviews the antibullying policy with the students, it suspends the offender according to the student code of conduct, and it provides counseling for your child. In this case, if the bullying were to continue, my opinion—as an expert in education administration and supervision—would be that the school did act reasonably even though the bullying continued. This type of intervention by the school helps to establish its level of liability.

The Michigan case is typical of the progression of a lawsuit: The plaintiff alleges that the school was notified that his son was being bullied. The child may have reported being bullied to his teacher, counselor, or other school official, but nobody in charge did anything about it or did too little too late and the bullying continued, leading to injury or death. The parent may claim that he called the school, reported the bullying, and that the school official said she would investigate, but nothing happened.

Keep in mind that every case is unique, and you cannot generalize from this example to your own. If you do reach for a legal solution to the problem, you will be faced with the task of clearly describing the bullying situation, what you communicated to the school, how and when you communicated to the school, whom you spoke with, what the school did as a result of your report, and the extent to which the bullying situation changed—if at all. If you have documented all of that information as you learned to do in chapters three and four, this will be easy for you to do when you engage an attorney or an expert in education administration and supervision.

Legally, the question will always be whether the school's actions were reasonable. This is where your written documentation is so important. Without it, the school may even claim that the initial bullying was never reported to anyone and that as a result, the school had no duty to do anything out of the ordinary to protect your child from harm. Your documentation will stand up in a court of law and can bridge this gap: *as a result of the school not intervening, my child was injured.*

A school can't just do something and say, "We did what we could." It has to check to make sure the intervention worked. If not, it has to try something else. Legally, the question is whether a school's actions were reasonable.

WHAT HAPPENS WHEN YOU PURSUE A LAWSUIT?

If you decide to sue your child's school for failing to protect her, it is important that an education expert consult with your attorney to review the case, develop an unbiased opinion, write an expert report, and testify in court.

Be ready for your lawsuit to take on the atmosphere of a stage production—and know that all of it will become a matter of public record. When there is a complaint and an answer, attorneys begin to "set the stage" with props that will be viewed by the "audience." Attorneys want the jurors (or the judge) to see certain issues (the props) under the brightest spotlight possible—with all the glitz and fanfare they can muster. Your attorney is your child's advocate. The attorney for the board of education is its advocate.

In Phoebe Prince's case, those props became clearer in the months leading up to the trial of the students who were charged in her death. The prosecutor, Elizabeth Farris, was expected to argue that the accused students violated Phoebe's civil rights when they called her an "Irish slut" and that their treatment of her interfered with her right to an education.[15] Lawyers for two of the defendants asked for medical records that they believed would portray Phoebe as having a long history of mental illness, including two suicide attempts before she took her own life.[16] To be sure, the defense will set up roadblocks like this to create doubt in a jury's mind. But in the end, proving a case against a school hinges on these questions:

- Did the school act appropriately and reasonably to protect the child from harm?
- Did the school act within the standard of professional care in the field of education administration and supervision, under the circumstances?

This is the crux of the matter, and it is what you want to discuss with your legal team. When I testify in court about my opinion, the jury or judge weighs the credibility of my testimony as an expert, the credibility of the other side's expert, and the credibility of the witnesses. After that, the jury or judge renders a verdict.

The jury will consider the amount and type of intervention a school provided to your child, as told through the testimony of expert witnesses. This will determine the extent of the school's liability and the jury's eventual verdict. If the school ignored the bullying after having knowledge of it and the bullying intensified, the school will be more culpable than if it knew about the bullying and intervened to some degree to stop it. This matter of degree is important—this is what the education experts will discuss in their testimonies, and it's what the jury will consider in rendering a verdict. If the jury believes that the school did all that it could to stop the bullying—even if the bullying continued anyway—it will likely hand up a verdict in favor of the school. If, on the other hand, the jury is persuaded that what the school did was not enough and that more should have and could have been done to end the bullying, it will likely side with the plaintiff.

A lawsuit against a Wisconsin school district, claiming that school officials were responsible for a girl's injuries because the district did not follow its own antibullying policies, illustrates the point.

RaChell Morenweiser was popular with her friends at Park Falls High School. She got good grades. A standout on her track team, RaChell pole-vaulted and threw shot put. But neither her friendships nor her bright future were of any comfort to her when a text message circulated falsely claiming that RaChell had been raped.

For RaChell, it was the culmination of two years of agony that included sexual harassment and cruel posts on her Facebook wall like "You suck at life" and "You should just die and go to hell," according to court filings.

Unable to cope with it anymore, RaChell shot herself in the stomach. Her attempt on her own life, however, was unsuccessful. The bullet entered her spine, rendering her a paraplegic.

Three months later, RaChell's parents filed suit against the Chequamegon School District, alleging that it failed to take action despite the parents' repeated efforts to bring their daughter's bullying to the attention of the district and law enforcement officials.

It would appear that RaChell's mother and stepfather, Jacqueline and Timothy Kennedy, followed many of the steps suggested in this book, notifying the school and taking their complaints up the chain of command. According to the lawsuit, Tim Kennedy—himself a teacher at another school in the district—told RaChell's guidance counselor two years earlier about the bullying. The counselor, Katherine Rybak, promised to tell RaChell's teachers about it, but she never did—in violation of district policies. Later that year, the Kennedys asked for a meeting with Principal Todd Lindstrom to discuss the bullying, but Lindstrom refused. Failing that, RaChell's parents met with the school resource officer, who brought the bullies together and warned them that he would charge them with disorderly conduct if the behavior continued. Tim Kennedy then went to the chief of police, who quickly arranged a meeting with Kennedy, the principal, and the counselor. Kennedy's suit alleges that instead of discussing his daughter's case, the school officials cautioned him to stop accusing them of not doing their jobs and implied that a job action could be taken against him.

Undaunted, the Kennedys continued to complain to the principal and the superintendent about the bullying, which intensified. RaChell's mother showed Lindstrom text messages from another student bragging about having harassed RaChell; Lindstrom accused RaChell of sending the messages. The Kennedys also notified Lindstrom, Rybak, and Superintendent Mark Luoma about the Facebook messages, but according to the Kennedys' suit, the three failed to do anything about the messages, in violation of district policies.

During this period, Tim Kennedy received two formal written disciplines in connection with his complaints about RaChell's harassment.

The suit maintains that Rybak, Lindstrom, and Luoma were "deliberately indifferent"—that term again—to RaChell's plight, depriving her of educational opportunities.[17] In this case, as with all suits against schools where bullying is involved, the two key questions will be applied: *Did the school act appropriately and reasonably to protect the child from harm? Did the school act within the standard of professional care in the field of education administration and supervision, under the circumstances?* Remember that a jury will want to know whether the school ignored the bullying after knowing about it or if it intervened to stop it. If it did intervene, then to what degree did it do so? The facts presented on these issues will determine the outcome of the case.

SIGN OF THINGS TO COME

How would your daughter feel if five boys repeatedly ganged up on her and called her fat and ugly? How would it make you feel if the school's response was, "Boys will be boys"? And how angry would it make you if your daughter was so upset by it all that she threw away her lunch every day and developed an eating disorder? Angry enough to sue?

Mary V., as court documents identify her, was. In August 2010, the board of Pittsburgh's public schools approved the settlement of her suit claiming that her daughter was subjected to peer bullying and harassment about her weight and had to enter an inpatient treatment program for anorexia nervosa because "her weight was dangerously low."

The suit alleged that by the time Mary V. went to the school about it, school officials already knew about the boys' abusive behavior toward her daughter but failed to tell her about it and do something to put an end to the teasing. The girl's guidance counselor responded to Mary V.'s initial complaint by saying, "Boys will be boys," and adding, "They must really like her if they are teasing her."

Mary V. settled out of court for $55,000. The boys eventually received a one-day suspension.[18] In many people who develop anorexia, the eating disorder is a symptom of underlying issues. Kids who are emotionally fragile are already susceptible to eating disorders, suicide, and other issues. A school needs to be especially diligent when implementing its antibullying policies if it knows about a student's emotional issues. These kids, with just one more mean word from a classmate, can be pushed over the edge.

This lawsuit is the first of its kind and provides a hint about what's over the horizon regarding legal action in light of bullying. We will see many more lawsuits of this type in the coming years as a result of the attention that has been drawn to serious medical consequences and suicides allegedly caused by bullying.

In all suits against schools where bullying is involved, two key questions will be applied:

- *Did the school act appropriately and reasonably to protect the child from harm?*
- *Did the school act within the standard of professional care in the field of education administration and supervision, under the circumstances?*

GROUNDBREAKING CASE

An important U.S. Supreme Court decision may give you the power to take action in court and seek damages against a school that fails to act appropriately, reasonably, and within the standard of professional care in the field of education administration. If your child's school ignores bullying, and your child is effectively denied an education, you can sue the school. The court allows monetary punishment for such inaction on the part of the school.

A fifth grader, LaShonda Davis, "was allegedly the victim of a prolonged pattern of sexual harassment by one of her fifth-grade classmates at Hubbard Elementary School, a public school in Monroe County Georgia," the 1999 U.S. Supreme Court opinion said.[19]

LaShonda's mom said that her daughter told her and her teacher that a boy in her class was relentlessly taunting her with sexual innuendo and simulated sexual acts. LaShonda's mother reported the incidents to school officials, including the principal, the court said.

As the girl's high grades dropped, her father discovered that she had written a suicide note. She was ten years old. LaShonda's parents filed a complaint with local law enforcement, her harasser was arrested, and the harassment finally ended when the boy pleaded guilty to sexual battery.

The damage to LaShonda had manifested itself as interference with her education—a right that every student has. Her grades dropped, and she missed many days of school because of the harassment.

LaShonda's family filed suit against the school district and its officials under federal Title IX, which bans sexual discrimination in schools receiving federal money. The lower federal courts said that the law, while covering school officials who engaged in sexual discrimination, did not include student-on-student harassment.

In a five-to-four decision, the Supreme Court reversed the lower courts' decisions, recognizing the family's right to sue under Title IX but making sure the grounds for suing were narrow and to the point. The ruling applies to students severely bullied in school through sexual harassment. Justice Sandra Day O'Connor wrote the majority opinion:

> We consider here whether a private damages action may lie against the school board in cases of student-on-student harassment. [Note: The court did not distinguish what type of harassment. LaShonda's harassment involved bullying of a sexual nature.] We conclude that it may, but only where the funding recipient (a school receiving federal funds) acts with deliberate indifference to known acts of harassment in its programs or activities. Moreover, we conclude that such an action will lie only for harassment that is so severe, pervasive, and objectively offensive that it effectively bars the victim's access to an educational opportunity or benefit.[20]

School districts can be liable if they ignore severe harassment that prevents a student from getting an education. In her opinion, Justice O'Connor rejected the school district's contention that the ruling would mean every bully would have to be expelled (the school district used the word *bully*):

> We stress that our conclusion here—that [school districts] may be liable for their deliberate indifference to known acts of peer sexual harassment—does not mean that [districts] can avoid liability only by purging their schools of actionable peer harassment or that administrators must engage in particular disciplinary action. We thus disagree with [the Monroe school district's] contention that, if Title IX provides a cause of action for student-on-student harassment, "nothing short of expulsion of every student accused of misconduct involving sexual overtones would protect school systems from liability or damages." . . . In fact, as we have previously noted, courts

should refrain from second-guessing the disciplinary decisions made by school administrators.[21]

Title IX states, "No person in the United States shall, on the basis of sex, be excluded from participation in, be denied the benefits of, or be subjected to discrimination under any education program or activity receiving federal financial assistance."[22] It included no private right to file suit, however, until this Supreme Court decision.

WHAT YOU'LL NEED

If you decide to consult an attorney about your child's bullying situation, you should have very clear documentation that she was denied access to an educational opportunity or benefit. In addition to the carefully scripted story of what the other kids were doing to bully her, you will need to show what her grades were and what activities she engaged in at school before the bullying. Next, you will need to document that this all changed after the bullying began. She may have experienced a drop in grades, she may have stayed out of school for a significant amount of time because of the bullying, she may not have been able to join a sports team because of her lower grades and/or attendance record, or she may not have been able to benefit from some aspect of the education offered at her school because of the bullying. Next, you will need to prove that the school acted deliberately indifferent to the actual knowledge that your child was being bullied. This is where the careful documentation you learned to prepare in chapters three and four pays off. Your attorney will want to know when and how the school was notified that your child was being bullied and what it did about it.

Did the school act swiftly to stop the bullying when it knew it was taking place? What did the school do, and was it effective—did the bullying stop or continue? If it continued, the response was not effective and the school may be held liable. Once the attorney defines the school district's duty, then she will review whether the district breached that duty. This is where your recordkeeping is vital. You have the information from your child about what was happening, you have the story written out in a script, you have a record of whom you spoke with at the school and what you said, you have a copy of the thank-you letter you sent to the principal with an outline of what he said he would do to stop the bullying, and you have information that indicates that the bullying is still taking place. Your attorney will review all of this with you and make a determination as to whether the school breached its duty to protect your child.

If the school did nothing, it is likely that it breached its duty. If the school did something but its actions did not end the bullying, it may have breached its duty. This is where an education expert needs to be engaged to render an opinion—based on his or her education, training, and personal and professional background—as to whether the school met its duty. If there was a breach of duty, then the next question would be whether your child was harmed. Absence from school and lower grades because of bullying might mean that your child was denied access to her educational program because of the school's breach of duty to protect her from bullying. Your attorney needs to argue that the breach of duty created a climate in the school in which bullying thrived, to the harm of your child. The jury has to understand and believe what happened before it can render a verdict.

If you do decide to visit or call an attorney to discuss whether the pursuit of a civil suit against the school would be advisable, your attorney will want to engage the services of an education expert who can review the case and render an opinion as to whether the school acted reasonably under the circumstances or whether it breached the standard of professional practice in the field of education administration and supervision. When I am engaged by attorneys (of both plaintiffs and defendants) all over the country on this topic, I don't advocate for one side or the other; I review the issues and render an opinion based upon my education, training, and professional experience. Advocacy is the job of an attorney. Rendering an unbiased opinion based upon a careful examination of the facts is the job of an expert.

CHAPTER SEVEN

BULLYING ON THE CYBER PLAYGROUND

KEYCEPT: The effects of cyberbullying can be more severe than those of "traditional" bullying because a child who is targeted may see no escape. Because of the scope of the Internet, there can be many more witnesses to cyberbullying. This form of bullying creates a different type of problem because kids who use computers and cell phones to harass another child can't see or hear the effects of their actions right away and can do it anonymously.

You can do a lot to protect your child from cyberbullying. Legally, though, this is still a gray area. When your child is bullied through the Internet or other electronic means, it can be harder to hold the school accountable because the bullying doesn't occur on school grounds. If the bullying involves the use of a school computer in the library, the school can be held to its policy governing the use of computers in school; but when the bullying originates from a cell phone in a child's bedroom, the school often can't be held directly responsible. Some states require schools to include cyberbullying in their antibullying policies, but mandates differ from state to state. Parents can be held accountable for their children's online activities if those activities are against the law.

What started as a classic situation of bullying in school—dirty looks and obscene insults in the hallways—ended as a horrific assault on Katie over the Internet and through text messages. Katie's mom became frightened for her eighth-grade daughter's safety when these kids started following and harassing the 14-year-old down the small-town streets of Peru, New York. Her fear was compounded by dismay when she asked the school and police for help but got nothing but the runaround. And all the while, Katie became more and more sad—the victim of an increasingly brutal cyberattack.

"I felt so helpless," Katie's mom told a local reporter who documented the family's odyssey. "They should have protected her more."[1]

The problems started when Katie and another girl liked the same boy. The other girl and her friends called Katie a whore and a slut, bothered her at school, and followed her around town. Katie fought back, but her mother simply told Katie to ignore it. That didn't end it. It got to be so bad that Katie stopped going to her brother's ball games because the girls who taunted her would be there.

Weeks passed, and Katie became quiet and emotionally fragile. Her father contacted the school and asked if Katie's lunch period could be switched. But the school didn't follow through and the lunch period wasn't changed.

As time went on, Katie spiraled downward into despair. She no longer wanted to go to school. Her grades dropped—something she could ill afford because her marks weren't all that strong to start with. That's when her mother decided to take a look at Katie's My-Space profile—and she cried at what she saw.

Katie's account had been hacked. A phony profile featured Katie's picture, her cell phone number, and a caption that read, "I work on the corners . . . hoe-4-life."[2] The students who set up the profile left cruel comments about Katie's body and appearance, threatened physical violence against her, and boasted of having pushed Katie around physically at school. Perhaps the worst part of it was that Katie knew all of this—but was too embarrassed to tell her parents about it. In chapter three, we talked about why your child doesn't always share information with you. Many children are at a developmental period in their life in which they are searching for independence—and not confiding in you is a way of exercising that search. Some kids are just afraid to approach their parents for fear of being embarrassed if their parents go to the school about the problem.

Katie's mother did what she thought she could. She contacted MySpace, which took down the profile within a day. She called the parents of the girls who had set up the fake profile; the parents denied that their kids were involved. (This is the usual defense mechanism: *Not my child. I know what she's doing on the computer.* In reality, they probably don't really know—or don't know enough.) She asked the school to set up a meeting with the resource officer and the families of the girls, but again, the school never followed through. She filed a complaint with the state police, but she heard nothing more about it. She twice suggested moving to a different district, but Katie refused to let her tormenters win that way. Katie wanted to hold her ground, but in reality, she was losing control of the situation.

When a person is being bullied and doesn't know how to combat it, doesn't go to her parents because she's embarrassed, expects her school to do something but is disappointed when it doesn't, and is hurting on the inside, it's not unusual for her to act out. Katie told her mother that she felt as if her own school didn't come to her defense because she wasn't worth it. Not surprisingly, Katie got in trouble on school grounds after a dance (reports don't specify what the trouble involved), was suspended, and was charged with trespassing. Until now, she had nothing of this sort on her record.[3]

Victims of bullying often experience years of constant anxiety, low self-esteem, and insecurity. And yet, as we have seen in so many stories throughout this book, bullying problems are too often ignored or taken lightly. When a child feels as if nobody wants to help her, it can manifest itself in violence, petty criminal activity, falling grades, or social isolation. The effects of cyberbullying, in which abusive actions are seen by hundreds of people and the group dynamic snowballs rapidly, can devastate a child and her family. When children take their own lives because of having been bullied in cyberspace, we know it's a problem that has gone too far.

TAKE THESE FAMILIAR STEPS
TO FIGHT CYBERBULLYING

Cyberbullying is one of the fastest-growing problems facing school administrators, lawmakers, and law enforcement officials. Broadly defined, cyberbullying is use of the computer or other electronic device to intimidate, threaten, or humiliate another person. It is an aggressive, intentional act of cruelty, carried out either by an individual or by a group of people, against a person who cannot easily defend himself because of the nature of the media used to attack. Most commonly, cyberbullying takes place on the Internet among students from the same school or neighborhood. One of the biggest difficulties in fighting cyberbullying lies in the difficulty in tracking its occurrences.

Would you be surprised to know that Peru Middle School accepted no responsibility for Katie's problems? When interviewed by a local newspaper about Katie's story, Peru school superintendent

A. Paul Scott dismissed the problem: "There are some types of interactions between and among students off campus . . . and there are frequently phone, texting, e-mail messages and instant messaging, and sometimes those matters can spill into school."[4]

Remember—you can't count on the school; some schools circle the wagons when they are threatened with exposure. That's what happened here. The superintendent deflected the school's responsibility. He started from the perspective that the behavior was all occurring outside of the school and sometimes spilled into the school. But he didn't mention that the school had been contacted by Katie's father, who had asked him to change her lunch assignment to get Katie away from her tormentors. He didn't address the issues that had occurred at school-sponsored sports events where kids had bullied Katie. He didn't talk about the school's antibullying policy, nor did he specify whether it covered cyberbullying.

It is going to take years of legal cases to pin down schools' responsibility to protect children from cyberbullying. For now, the primary questions revolve around the degree to which cyberbullying interferes with a student's educational opportunities.

In Katie's case, it would appear that the interference was significant. Katie's grades dropped—supporting the argument that the behavior of these bullies interfered with her right to an education. This could be grounds for a civil rights lawsuit. As we learned in chapter six, if the school has a duty to protect your child, was notified about the bullying, and didn't act appropriately and reasonably and within the standard of professional practice—and your child's education suffered as a result—the school may be liable.

Cyberbullying, though, is so pervasive and insidious, it will take more than strong-willed schools and lawmakers to stop its spread; the victim and her family have to attack it head-on as well. That means following the same steps covered previously in this book:

talk with your child, talk with the school, document the school's response with a thank-you letter, and follow through as far as you need to until the harassment against your child stops.

Let's take a look at what Katie and her family could have done differently.

KATIE'S MOTHER TOLD HER DAUGHTER TO IGNORE THE PROBLEM

We already know that this is not the way to deal with onslaughts of misbehavior from kids who are mean-spirited. Remember the teenage brain? It's on its way to adulthood, but the ride takes many twists and turns of emotional conflict along the way. At this age, kids are forming their identity, and sometimes that results in kids getting emotionally hurt. The girls who hacked Katie's MySpace account thought nothing of the consequences of their actions.

KATIE'S PARENTS DID NOT COMMUNICATE EFFECTIVELY WITH THEIR DAUGHTER

There can be many reasons why Katie didn't tell her parents about the depth of the harassment that she experienced—primary among them is likely that she didn't know how to approach them. And maybe her parents didn't establish an effective way of communicating with Katie if their initial response was to dismiss all that was beginning to happen around her. Following the steps in chapter three will help you to communicate effectively with your child so that you can communicate effectively with the school.

KATIE'S MOTHER DID NOT DOCUMENT HER DAUGHTER'S TORTURE AND THE SCHOOL'S RESPONSE TO IT

Katie told her mother what was happening, who was bullying her, and where it was happening. Yet her mother didn't contact the school. She didn't know the school's policy about this type of behavior and that these kids could be disciplined. In her frustration, she just told Katie to ignore her tormenters and the behavior would stop. If Katie's mother had gone to the school right away with the information, the school would have been notified of what was happening to her daughter and would have had a duty to intervene effectively to protect Katie. And if it didn't, Katie's mother could have held the school accountable to protect her daughter.

Cyberbullying is one of the fastest-growing problems facing school administrators, lawmakers, and law enforcement officials. It will take years of legal cases to establish schools' responsibility in this area.

A NEW WAY OF SOCIALIZING

Kids socialize very differently these days. A lot of socializing takes place on the Internet—a world that can be difficult for you to monitor. The Internet is remote, and unless your child shares the information with you, it will be impossible to know that your child is being subjected to bullying online.

As a parent, you know that your child spends a lot of time involved with media—both traditional and social media. But do you really know how much time? And do you know the risks associated with certain media for bullying and being bullied?

According to a Henry J. Kaiser Family Foundation study released in January 2010, 8- to 18-year-olds spend more time with media than any other activity besides (maybe) sleeping—an average of more than seven and a half hours a day, seven days a week.[5] The TV shows they watch, video games they play, websites they visit, and songs they listen to are a large part of their lives. They get a continuous stream of messages, which are unfiltered in most circumstances. The question is this: are these messages—received and sent—promoting positive relationships and attitudes toward others?

Among all 8- to 18-year-olds, the average amount of time spent on just the computer during each day tripled from 27 minutes in 1999 to 1 hour and 29 minutes in 2009. Sure, kids are accessing websites to assist with schoolwork, but a lot more is taking place. One quarter of that time online is spent in social networks, such as MySpace and Facebook. Almost 20 percent more is spent with instant messaging and email.[6] Sociologists say that all this use of electronic communication gives rise to a growing concern: kids don't take the time to play with each other anymore. Without unstructured free time, they don't learn to connect and care. When they don't spend time with friends, they don't learn empathy. They do, however, learn about indirect aggression and violence from video games, and sometimes they model the behavior they see from their peers in cyberspace.

No doubt your child has embraced the Internet and social media for many positive uses—communicating with friends and making new friends, seeking information, and creating his own websites and blogs. But with this activity comes an increased likelihood that the Internet is also being used against your child, where others are sending him hurtful information or images. And it's not just computers; advances in smartphone technology make it possible for a bully to use his cell phone to harass others. These phones can be used to send text messages and to take pictures and videos that can be sent to other cell phones or posted instantly on social networking sites—long before the target of those messages will know what happened.

Unfortunately, this means that kids can be bullied even when they're not at school. This leaves your child few, if any, places to hide. Just like Katie, your child may be afraid to confide in you about the problem she is having with a classmate who says that she is a "slut" in text messages she is sending to dozens of her friends at school. Your child may be embarrassed or may fear that you will restrict the use of her computer or take her cell phone away.

As a parent, you can make a difference. Children whose parents make an effort to limit media use—through example, setting limits, and the environment parents create in the home—spend less time with media, on average, than their peers.[7] With that comes a reduced risk of children being hurt or hurting others in cyberspace.

THE MANY FACES OF CYBERBULLYING

How many ways can your child be cyberbullied? As technology advances, so will the myriad ways kids can use it to be cruel to one another. Here are a few examples of the dangers that may await your child.

EMAIL

Fourteen-year-old Shruti struggled with her weight. The kids in her class circulated malicious emails that made fun of the way she looked—and when she saw them, she refused to go back to school. She asked her parents to send her to another school.

Her parents talked with the principal, who was quick to identify the students who had poked fun of Shruti. He made them apologize—after which Shruti agreed to come back to school—and he was not bashful about the school's responsibility to take charge of the situation: "It's high time we accept cyberbullying and other misuse of the Internet by children and take action," he said. "We have to teach children to differentiate between right and wrong while using technology."[8]

It so happens that this school was in India, which illustrates how serious the problem is worldwide. Increasingly, students the world over are using cyberspace to bully vulnerable students, and these bullied students are sometimes using cyberspace to then take revenge.

WEBSITES

Beneath a heading that read "She's queer because," students posted their own crude epithets about eighth grader Kylie Kenney. The website—called *Kill Kylie Incorporated*—had been set up by some of her fellow students. Kylie learned of it only when a classmate asked if she had seen the website. She hadn't, nor could she understand why someone would do such a thing.

Beginning with the day the website was set up, Kylie endured two years of relentless cyber- and face-to-face bullying from classmates. "I had no escape," she said later. "Everything followed me to school." It got to the point where these mean kids used Kylie's screen name to pretend to be her online and make sexually suggestive remarks about Kylie's teammates on the field hockey team. They even asked her teammates out on dates, posing as Kylie all the while. Nine months later, the students behind the website were finally discovered. Two students were suspended, and the police filed charges of harassment against one person who had made a death threat online against Kylie.[9]

This is but one variety of the most popular strategy among tech-savvy bullies: directly attacking the victim through the Internet while remaining completely anonymous. As Kylie learned, because the website is public, anyone can come across it; as a result, it has high potential to embarrass the person it targets.

SOCIAL NETWORKING SITES

Another case took place in Clinton, Missouri, where a teenage girl was accused of slandering another girl on Facebook. She used a fake identity to set up a Facebook page that targeted a romantic rival. The abusive behavior caused the victim significant stress that affected her studies and her school attendance.[10]

The case is one of countless instances of the use of phony pages on Facebook or MySpace that are used to harass children or stir up trouble between friends. *Bullying by proxy* involves unleashing an attack on one victim in the name of someone else by either using a fake identity or pretending to be someone else. The latter is doubly cruel because it essentially "frames" an innocent person. Sometimes, the attacker will use the name of the intended victim to send out rude messages to each of the victim's friends.

A slightly different twist on the use of social networking to bully others involved more than two dozen students from a Seattle middle school. At the heart of the incident was a Facebook page that students could become a "fan" of if they didn't like the intended victim. Though the page was removed within 24 hours, 28 kids had joined it—and all 28 were suspended anywhere from two to eight days depending on their level of involvement. In this case, the school had an antibullying program and a zero tolerance policy, and administrators knew that they had a responsibility to get involved when an incident creates a significant disruption at the school. After the incident, the principal discussed appropriate use of the Internet and online safety at student assemblies and in meetings with parents.[11]

TEXT AND VIDEO MESSAGES

Text and photos sent from one cell phone to another can be harmless or they can be mean-spirited. And sometimes, what starts out as harmless can turn sour. In Bothell, Washington, two high school cheerleaders used their cell phones to snap nude pictures of one another; one of the two then sent her own pictures to her then-boyfriend's cell phone. But—like email—once a picture is sent out, there's no telling whose hands it can wind up in—or what website it can get posted on. And the girl who sent the picture to her boyfriend learned that lesson the hard way. It may have been a case of male bravado, or it may have been a form of bullying if the relationship went bad, but her boyfriend sent the picture to other students. It circulated quickly, making its way to members of the football team. School officials suspended the two cheerleaders after obtaining the photos, and child pornography charges were brought against the two. The girls' parents sued the district, unhappy that their daughters were disciplined but not the students who had received and resent the photos.[12]

Today, a lot of socializing takes place on the Internet. The important question to ask is this: do these interactions promote positive relationships and attitudes toward others?

MEASURING THE EXTENT OF CYBERBULLYING

These stories represent a fraction of what occurs online every day. But what is the real scope of cyberbullying? That's difficult to know for sure. Research studies have produced different answers, depending on the definition of cyberbullying that is used, the ages and characteristics of children surveyed, and the time frame involved. According to one survey of kids in grades four through eight, 42 percent of children have been cyberbullied and 35 percent have been threatened online.[13]

In a 2009 Cox Communications survey, 13- to 18-year-olds were asked how often they had ever been involved in cyberbullying:

- 15 percent said that they had been cyberbullied online.

- 10 percent said that they had been cyberbullied by cell phone.
- 7 percent said that they had cyberbullied another person online.
- 5 percent said that they had cyberbullied another person by cell phone.[14]

A study by Fight Crime: Invest in Kids investigated how often children (6- to 11-year-olds) and teens (12- to 17-year-olds) had been cyberbullied, as well as the nature of the cyberbullying. One-third of the teens and one-sixth of the children reported that someone had said threatening or embarrassing things about them online during the previous year. Moreover, the investigation found the following:

- 10 percent of teens and 4 percent of preteens were threatened online with physical harm.
- Preteens received as many email threats at school as they did in their homes.
- About one in six who were threatened online said nothing to anyone about it.[15]

In one academic study, 6 percent of students in grades six through eight said that they had been cyberbullied more than once in the past couple of months.[16] In another study, 8 percent of middle schoolers had cyberbullied others in the last 30 days and 18 percent had done so at some point during their lifetimes.[17]

That's a lot of bullying. And, as with most self-reported surveys, the figures are probably lower than what really takes place.

Some studies have found that more girls than boys are involved in cyberbullying, but others have reported similar rates among boys and girls. Whether girls or boys, cyberbullies enjoy the cloak of anonymity that the Internet gives them to spread their venom; in fact, when middle school students were asked in one study about the identity of the person who cyberbullied them, almost half—48 percent—said that they didn't know. Among those who did know who was behind their harassment, the following was the case:[18]

- 52 percent identified another student at school.
- 36 percent said that they had been cyberbullied by a friend.
- 13 percent said that they had been cyberbullied by a sibling.[19]

Cyberbullying appears to occur more often during the teenage years, but it is not unusual even among elementary-age kids.

A PRIMER ON THE CYBER PLAYGROUND

The cyberworld takes many forms. Knowing the ins, the outs, and the jargon will help you protect your child and make the school accountable.

Cyberbullying is accomplished in many ways, including the following:

- *Bash boards* are online bulletin boards where people can post whatever they like about a person or a topic—usually something mean-spirited or malicious.
- *Denigration*, also known as *dissing* or *disrespecting*, is when a person uses electronic methods to spread rumors, gossip, or false statements to damage a person's reputation or relationships.

- *Exclusion* is when someone intentionally excludes someone else from an online group.
- *Flaming* is an online fight that involves the use of hostile, insulting, or vulgar messages. These messages can be posted to a private or public online group. The victim is said to be *flamed.*
- *Griefing* is causing grief to members of an online community; sometimes, it refers to intentional disruption of another player in game play.
- *Happy slapping* is when an unsuspecting victim is physically attacked by one or more people while another person films or takes pictures of the incident; the images or video are then posted online or sent to others by cell phone. Often, the defense of the attackers is that it was only a prank.
- *Harassment* is straightforward: the cyberbully repeatedly sends insulting, hurtful, or rude messages to a victim.
- *Images and videos* are fast-growing concerns because the camera phone has become ubiquitous. Pictures and movies can be taken of unsuspecting victims in places like bathrooms or locker rooms and emailed to people or published on sites like YouTube, MySpace, or Facebook.
- *Impersonation*—described earlier as *bullying by proxy*—is when someone pretends to be another person; not unlike identity theft, this is usually accomplished by breaking into someone's account or stealing a password. This form of cyberbullying can cause irreparable harm to a victim's reputation and friendships.
- *Malicious code* can be either a virus that is sent with the intention of damaging or harming someone's computer, or software that is used to spy on the victim.

- *Online polls* are sent by text messaging or are posted on sites like Facebook. They ask questions that can hurt another person or ruin someone's reputation, such as "What girl do you love to hate?" or "Who do you think Roxanne has slept with?"
- *Outing* is when confidential or embarrassing information is published online.
- *Sexting* is the act of sending sexually explicit messages or photos between mobile phones; it can lead to harassment when those messages or photos fall into the wrong person's hands.
- *Text wars* and *text attacks* are when several people send the victim hundreds of harassing emails or text messages. Aside from the emotional toll this takes, the victim's cell phone charges can be costly.
- *Trickery* is when a person lures another person into revealing secrets and then puts that information online; it also can involve tricking a person out of account information, such as a password.[20]

HOW TO KNOW IF YOUR CHILD IS CYBERBULLIED

It's not always apparent that your child is being bullied, and it's not always easy for her to discuss it with you. But if you know the signs that might indicate that she is being cyberbullied, you can apply your effective-communication skills to find out what's going on.

Here's what you need to look for that may indicate that your child is a victim of cyberbullying. Any one symptom alone does not necessarily mean cyberbullying is taking place, but be concerned if a combination of a few is occurring—especially any that involve the use of the computer or cell phone:

- excessive computer use (or alternatively, avoiding the computer, cell phone, and other devices)
- the avoidance of conversations about the use of the computer and other devices
- anxiety when using the computer, checking text messages, or using instant messaging
- lack of interest in checking cell phone messages
- depression
- antisocial behavior or withdrawal from family and friends or school or other activities
- increased sadness, anger, frustration, and worry, as well as reduced tolerance
- declining grades
- changes in eating habits (particularly the onset of anorexia or bulimia)
- troubled sleep or nightmares

If you suspect that your child is being cyberbullied, you'll also want to look for signs of her being bullied in the traditional way at school or social activities. (The same is true the other way around—if your child is being bullied at school, watch for signs of cyberbullying as well.)

You also should be aware of signs that your child may be cyberbullying others. Notice that some of these symptoms are the same as those to look for when you suspect that your child is being cyberbullied:

- excessive use of the computer and/or cell phone
- the avoidance of conversations about the use of the computer and cell phone
- previous episodes of bullying others or having been bullied

- a tendency to close computer applications or switch screens when you get near
- the use of multiple online accounts or an account that does not belong to your child
- unusual agitation if you restrict or deny access to the computer or cell phone

Children who are involved in cyberbullying are also very likely to be involved in traditional forms of bullying. In a study of middle school students, 61 percent of those who said that they were victims of cyberbullying also said that they had experienced traditional forms of bullying. Similarly, 55 percent of cyberbullies said that they had also bullied kids in other ways. Among the kids who had been both cyberbully and cybervictim, most had been involved in traditional forms of bullying—64 percent had been bullied, and 66 percent had bullied others.[21]

It's important to understand that cyberbullying is not a trend. Unfortunately, cyberbullying—like traditional bullying—is here to stay. So what can you do about it? Listen to the stories about cyberbullying and find the commonalities in them to understand it better—then get your hands dirty on a keyboard.

STAY A STEP AHEAD

For many of you, navigating the Internet or using a BlackBerry is something that you do every day and that comes naturally. For many more of you, this frontier is new and intimidating. But if you want to know what's going on in the cyberworld with your kids, you need to dive in yourself. Here are some ideas to help you get started.

PUT THE COMPUTER SOMEPLACE PUBLIC

If a computer in your home has Internet access, put it in a room that you visit frequently—and be sure that you can see the monitor.

BONE UP AND PRACTICE

Become Internet savvy and learn about computer applications and smartphone "apps." Knowing what you can do with a computer and a cell phone is critical to understanding the many dangers that await your child. Taking a class may help—and it may help you to be proactive in teaching younger children about the safe use of electronic communication.

JOIN SOCIAL NETWORKING WEBSITES

Knowing how these things work and how your child can access them is crucial. Create a user identity and spend time in chat rooms that your child might frequent. What are the discussions like? Are they appropriate? Used responsibly, social networking sites like Facebook can be an excellent way for kids to stay in touch and learn from one another. They become a risk to your child only when they are abused, so spending time online to understand the safety features that each site has to offer can help you protect your child.

BE THERE, EVEN WHEN YOU CAN'T

You can't spend every minute next to your child when she is online. Being able to communicate quickly with her when she is online can be the next best thing, especially if your child finds herself in an uncomfortable situation. Software exists to help your child report and document unhealthy and bullying situations that occur online. CyberBully Alert is one example of software that allows children to notify their parents in these situations and saves a screenshot for parents to use as documentation.

COMMUNICATE CONSISTENTLY WITH YOUR CHILD

Know when your child is going online; for younger children, asking permission to go online may be appropriate. Communicate proactively so that your child develops good online etiquette and behavior. These skills can be important if your child is threatened in the cyberworld. Remember—you want to keep the lines of communication with your child open so that he will come to you, rather than hide, when he experiences cyberbullying.

Here are some tips for talking with your child about cyberbullying:

- Educate your child about cyberbullying, and reinforce which types of online behavior are acceptable and which are not.
- Advise your child to give his cell phone number and personal email address only to trusted friends.
- Encourage your child to avoid opening emails from cyberbullies or responding to bullies through text messaging.
- Warn your child to talk with people in cyberspace only if he has met them in person.
- Suggest that your child block the bully from his cybersystems (you may have to contact your Internet and cell phone service providers to do this).

Talk with your child regularly about her online activities and experiences. Judiciously apply the fact-finding tips you learned in chapter three; if your child feels as if she is being judged or investigated, she may turn away from this conversation (and future conversations like it). Ask her about the activities of others that she may communicate with online. Review your child's instant messaging buddy list and Facebook friends on a regular basis and ask questions to make certain that he is communicating only with people that he actually knows.

Set clear expectations with your child about what he should do if he is the target of a bullying communication. Your child should tell you immediately, ignore or block the message (if possible), and understand how to report threatening incidents to your Internet service provider and how to report abuse to the website on which the incident occurred.

If you want to know what's going on in the cyberworld with your kids, you need to learn how to use the cyberworld yourself.

WHAT THE LAW SAYS ABOUT CYBERBULLYING

If this was your child, what would you think?

Your ninth-grade daughter comes home from school one day, upset that the assistant principal took her cell phone. The assistant principal went through her text messages, then handed the phone back and sent your daughter back to class. Along the way, he explained to her that a tenth-grade boy had been sending out crude, sexually explicit messages—and that your daughter was said to have been one of the people to get one of those messages. It turned out that she hadn't, but she was angry that she was accused and that her phone was searched.

This occurred in the Oak Harbor School District in Washington State, where at the beginning of the 2010–2011 school year, administrators began searching electronic devices on campus. The school's new antibullying policy allows administrators to review anything in a student's cell phone, including text messages, pictures, and videos. Facing a new state mandate to get tough on cyberbullies and sexting, the district said that its policy is meant to keep kids out of harm's way.

Some students protested what they perceived to be "an invasion of privacy," and some parents voiced concern that the school was taking over a parent's role. The superintendent said that the goal was to team up with parents in the name of keeping their children safe.[22]

Not all state laws require schools to include cyberbullying in their antibullying policies. In states where it is required, the school has to address it in its policy. While some schools hold parents responsible for monitoring their children's cyberbehavior during after-school hours, many schools have begun addressing the issue within their own walls. Laws in many states are changing rapidly, but at the time of this book's publication, here is what some state laws say about cyberbullying:

- *Arkansas* allows school officials to take action against students who cyberbully fellow students, even if the bullying did not originate or occur on school property.[23]
- *Idaho* passed "Jared's Law," under which school officials may suspend students who harass other students through the use of a computer or a telephone.[24]
- *Iowa* requires schools to develop anticyberbullying policies to protect students from bullying "in schools, on school property or at any school function or school-sponsored activity."[25]
- *Louisiana* can charge anyone age 18 or older who cyberbullies a younger person with "cyberstalking," punishable by a fine of $500 or six months in jail. Kids 17 and under who are caught cyberbullying must undergo counseling.[26]

- *New Jersey* recently amended its already-tough law to include bullying that takes place via "electronic communication." This gives schools the power to dole out punishment for actions that occur off of school grounds.[27]
- *Oregon* expanded the definition of cyberbullying in its laws to include actions that "substantially interfere" with a child's education.[28]
- *New York* signed an antibullying law in June 2010, but the law does not address cyberbullying.[29] A previous law, however, provides a system that enables police and school officials to investigate claims of cyberbullying, determine the circumstances of each occurrence, and prosecute or punish the offender.[30]
- *Vermont* added a $500 fine for cyberbullying offenses to its already-tough bullying laws.[31]

You can check on your state's current cyberbullying laws by visiting www.bullypolice.com.

If your state and school do not address the subject and your child is bullied off of school grounds through the use of electronic media, contact your local police or prosecutor to find out if there are laws that can be invoked to press charges. Also contact the police immediately if you think that your child's safety is in danger. This may include threats of violence, extortion, obscene or harassing calls, stalking, sexual exploitation, or photographic invasions of privacy. I'll talk more about this later in this chapter.

It's important to understand that because cyberbullying is such a new frontier, the laws that define and police it are, in many places, weak to nonexistent. Missouri recently updated its cyberbullying statute, addressing a gaping legal hole that swallowed the life of a teenage girl.

Megan Meier was a 13-year-old from Missouri who developed an online infatuation on MySpace with a boy named Josh Evans, who she believed was new in her town. In reality, "Josh" was a group of people—including two adults—intent on humiliating Megan because a friendship she had with another girl went sour. One of those adults was 48-year-old Lori Drew, the mother of that girl, who was angry about Megan "spreading lies" about her daughter, according to court testimony. The idea was to lure Megan into making disparaging comments about the girl, after which Drew would present the evidence to Megan's mother.

When Drew decided to end the ruse, "Josh" started to push away from Megan. The messages became increasingly mean. Josh's last email opined, "The world would be a better place without you."

Shortly after she read that message, Megan hanged herself.[32]

The media swooped into Megan's St. Louis suburb. Prosecutors looked to the law for the authority to charge the perpetrators with a crime, but there was no provision for them to rely on. Nobody in Missouri could be criminally prosecuted for sending threatening or harassing electronic messages to another person unless those messages were sent over the telephone. Eventually, the case was tried by a federal jury in California, where MySpace is located, and Drew was convicted on three misdemeanor counts of computer fraud for having misrepresented herself—a violation of the Computer Fraud and Abuse Act of 1986.

Megan's tragic death motivated the Missouri legislature to update the law to reflect modern means of communication. The governor created a task force whose sole purpose was to study and create laws about cyberbullying. As a result, the work of the Internet Harassment Task Force became an example for other states. Now, prosecution for harassment through any means of electronic communication is possible. In Missouri, such harassment carries the potential for felony charges that may carry a term of years in the penitentiary.

If your child's peers in school cyberbully her, get a copy of your school's antibullying policy. See if cyberbullying is covered and the extent to which your school can act. Hold the school accountable for protecting her from the harm of cyberbullying if, in fact, the school has a policy against it, defines its role in monitoring it, and specifies in the student code of conduct the steps that it will take to discipline violators. Practice what you've learned about effective communication with her to find out what's happening, and practice effective communication with the school if you find out that she is being bullied through cyberspace.

Increasingly, schools will automatically involve the police. The Chicago Board of Education passed a student code of conduct, effective with the 2010–2011 school year. Cyberbullies caught using cell phones or social networking websites to pick on classmates face mandatory suspension, possible expulsion, and a police investigation.[33]

Chicago school officials instituted tough rules that regulate student behavior not just during school hours, but also outside school hours, as well as off campus. The board now considers cyberbullying an offense as serious as burglary, aggravated assault, gang activity, or drug use. Students in Chicago who use computers or phones to bully others will be suspended for five to ten days and may be expelled. Details about any offense are automatically referred to Chicago police, who have the authority to charge students with criminal activity.[34]

Remember how in chapter two we talked about the fact that you can't always count on the school? Well, in Chicago, the rules are pretty tough—but the question remains: will Chicago schools adhere to their rules to protect kids from harm? Though a school may include cyberbullying in its policy, everything you have learned up until now still applies if you are to make the school follow through: You still have to know when bullying is occurring—whether it's the traditional or cyber type. You still have to be observant, ask questions, and know how to communicate effectively with your child to know what's happening. You still need to get behind the principal's office door, know what the school knows, and know what its policies are. You still need to communicate effectively with the school to make it end the bullying. And you have to become familiar with the cyberworld if you are really intent on understanding what is being done to your child.

SCHOOLS AND THE CYBER PLAYGROUND

Depending on the manner in which cyberbullying is occurring, school administrators may be in trouble if they do—or if they do not—respond.

Schools have been held liable for harm caused by on-campus harassment and bullying that resulted from educator negligence. However, the standards under which schools and educators can be held responsible vary from state to state. Certainly, schools have a duty to ensure that students are using school communications networks or mobile devices in a way that does not harm other students. The question that would be raised would be whether the school acted reasonably and prudently in light of what it knew.

If you file a civil lawsuit against your child's school for negligence and breach of its duty to protect your child, the factors that would be considered include the following: state law, the district's policies, the school's efforts to communicate those policies to students, the training of staff about those policies, the manner in which the district allows students to use its communications networks, the degree to which the district supervises and monitors students' use of those devices, and the procedures established for reporting and addressing cyberbullying concerns.

First, your attorney will need to establish that the school has a duty to protect your child under the specific circumstance. There may not be a duty under certain state laws and school policy for the school to police cyberbullying off campus. Next, your attorney will need to prove to a jury that the school knew that the bullying was taking place but didn't appropriately and effectively respond—and that the bullying continued or got worse. Finally, she will need to persuade the jury that the school's negligence caused harm to, or at least contributed to the harm of, your child.

As a parent of a child who is being cyberbullied, become familiar with state law and your school district's policies. You already know how to access these; read them to determine whether the situation affecting your child fits any of the descriptions of cyberbullying. If so, then you know how to address the issue by following the steps outlined in chapter four about communicating effectively with the school.

Because a significant amount of cyberbullying occurs off campus, the school may have less authority to respond to cyberbullying with a traditional disciplinary response, depending on state law and the local board of education's policies. You should know that for totally off-campus speech—that is, speech in which the only school connection is that students from the school are involved—school administrators cannot intervene unless there is a substantial and material threat of disruption to the educational process at the school. This standard is likely to be met only in cases that would justify contacting law enforcement officials.

There may be other off-campus cyberbullying situations, however, in which administrators may be compelled to respond. You may be able to hold the school accountable to respond in the following situations:

- A student takes a picture of another student at school, then posts it online in an abusive or unflattering manner.
- The cyberbullying is related to face-to-face bullying that occurs at school or at a school-sponsored activity.

You may discover that your school can't respond directly to a cyberbullying situation or can't impose discipline because the situation is not covered by state law and by the school board's policies against bullying. This can be very frustrating. Depending on the nature of the activity, you may be able to pursue the case with law enforcement officials (see the following section entitled "When to Go to Law Enforcement").

Even if the school cannot impose discipline on cyberbullies, there are many other ways that the school can help. You can ask an administrator to provide support and assistance to your child if he is cyberbullied. Given the psychological harm suffered by victims of bullying and cyberbullying and the impact on your child's well-being—as well as the possible impact on the school—you should be very clear with the principal that you would like to work together to deal with this situation and that you would very much appreciate an opportunity for your child to set up a series of regular appointments with the school psychologist to talk about what happened to him. You can use the script you learned about in chapter four, modify it to fit the cyberbullying circumstance, and contact the principal for assistance.

Remember—it's important to do your research first. Find out if the school has a responsibility, under state law, to have a policy that addresses cyberbullying. Next, contact the school for a copy of its antibullying policy and review the section on cyberbullying. Develop your narrative of what's happening to your child and relate it to the school's policy, if it is required to have one. If your state does not require your school to cover cyberbullying in its policy, contact the principal anyway and go through the story of what's happening. Ask for the assistance of the school. You might be surprised by a positive response. Let's hope so.

WHEN TO INVOLVE POLICE AND LAWYERS

Some cyberbullying is a violation of criminal law. As a general guide, law enforcement officials should be contacted whenever you become aware of cyberbullying that involves the following:

- death threats or threats of violence to your child or her property
- excessive intimidation or extortion
- threats or intimidation that involve bias, such as those based on race, religion, gender, or sexual orientation
- any evidence of sexual exploitation

Cyberbullying may also meet the legal standard for intentional torts, which are intentional wrongdoings. In most states, parents can be held financially liable for intentional torts committed by their children. This knowledge should be helpful to you if you have to contact the parents of the child who is cyberbullying your child. When those parents understand that they may be liable for what their child is doing on the Internet or over the cell phone, it is likely that they will cooperate in removing cyberbullying material or ensuring that their child stops the behavior.

Although the following elements are best determined by your attorney, you should know what they are so that you can have a full understanding of your child's rights and the legal sanctions that can be invoked against the child who hurts yours through cyberbullying.

The following are the commonly accepted legal elements for intentional torts:

DEFAMATION

- A false damaging statement was published.
- The statement identified the victim.
- The statement harmed the victim's reputation in the community (this includes the school community).
- The person committing the defamation did something that he should not have done.

Keep in mind that truth is a defense. If what a person said online is true, he can defend his actions.

INVASION OF PRIVACY

- A person publicly discloses a nonpublic detail of another person's private life, causing an effect that would be highly offensive to a reasonable person.
- A person is placed before the public in a false light that would be highly offensive to a reasonable person.

There are some defenses to accusations of invasion of privacy. If the facts are "newsworthy," they may be revealed, and if it is judged that the victim gave consent. Minors, however, are not capable of giving legal consent.

INTENTIONAL INFLECTION OF EMOTIONAL DISTRESS

- A person's intentional or reckless actions cause extreme distress.
- The actions must be outrageous and regarded as utterly intolerable in a civilized community.[35]

A number of lawsuits associated with cyberbullying have been filed. Lawsuits must meet the legal criteria for intentional torts, or they may be tossed out of court.

A Long Island judge dismissed a teenager's defamation suit against four classmates who had set up a Facebook page on which they joked that the girl used heroin and developed AIDS by having sex with animals in Africa.

The judge ruled that no reasonable person could believe that the statements were facts. "A reasonable reader, given the overall context of the posts, simply would not believe that the plaintiff contracted AIDS by having sex with a horse or a baboon or that she contracted AIDS from a male prostitute who also gave her crabs and syphilis"—he said, recounting the bullies' claims about her online—"or that [after] having contracted sexually transmitted diseases in such manner, she morphed into the devil." The judge said that the statements could be interpreted only as puerile attempts by adolescents to outdo each other.

In the same case, the judge also dismissed a negligent-supervision claim against the teenagers' parents, saying that a computer does not constitute, as required by New York case law, a "dangerous instrument." "To declare a computer a dangerous instrument in the hands of teenagers in an age of ubiquitous computer ownership would create an exception that would engulf the rule against parental liability," the judge concluded. The plaintiff sought $3 million for the damage to her reputation and character and another $3 million in punitive damages.[36]

The dismissal of the suit didn't make the teens' actions right; someone truly was hurt by what happened. But it apparently didn't meet the legal definition of intentional tort, which may or may not undergo new scrutiny as more cases of this newest form of bullying come to trial.

This whole area of cyberbullying is just appearing on the horizon at the time of this book's publication. State laws are not about whether schools have a duty to protect students from cyberbullying when it occurs off campus. Criminal laws are well established. However, even in the context of applying criminal law to prevent cyberbullying and protect kids from harm, what's unacceptable differs from jurisdiction to jurisdiction; case law is superseding old standards; and new laws are still being defined, tested, and revised as more of these cases are tried.

Not all state laws require schools to include cyberbullying in their antibullying policies. If your state requires it, your child's school has to address cyberbullying in its policy.

APPENDIX

This appendix includes scripts, letter samples, and other valuable resources that you can use to take action with your child's school, teacher, principal, and others. In addition to including information about communicating with state and federal education authorities, this appendix touches on what to think about and say if you need to contact a lawyer, and provides additional tips for stopping cyberbullies from reaching your child.

At the end of this appendix, you'll learn about a special website for readers of this book. This website is a rich resource of further reading about bullying and education law; it also provides links to other useful websites. You can also use this website to contact me directly with questions about bullying, how to find help, or how to handle your child's case.

The information in this appendix corresponds with the order of the information in this book, beginning with chapter three.

COMMUNICATING WITH YOUR CHILD (CHAPTER THREE)

In this section, you will find age-appropriate scripts for conversations with your child about bullying. These scripts set a tone that is nonjudgmental and that puts your emotions in check, putting your child at ease.

TALKING WITH YOUR CHILD ABOUT BEING BULLIED
Script for Talking with a Young Child

Once you have established that your child is being bullied, you can use the following script, with some modification. This script gives your child an opportunity to provide you with the information you need to act.

> PARENT: Who else was sitting at your table in the cafeteria when Joseph called you names?
>
> CHILD: I think Victoria and Matthew were there.
>
> PARENT: Was there a teacher in the cafeteria?
>
> CHILD: No.
>
> PARENT: Were any adults there?
>
> CHILD: Yes. Mrs. Murphy.
>
> PARENT: Who is she?
>
> CHILD: She's the cafeteria monitor.
>
> PARENT: Did she hear what Joseph said to you?
>
> CHILD: No, she didn't.
>
> PARENT: Did anyone else hear what he said to you?
>
> CHILD: No.

In other situations, your child might inform you that there was a teacher or cafeteria monitor near the table who heard what was said. If this is the case, ask your child if he can tell you the person's name. Also, get the last names of the other kids, if any, who heard or witnessed the bullying. Remember to record all of this information along with the day this happened.

PARENT: Did you tell anyone what Joseph said to you?

CHILD: Yes. I told Mrs. Johnston when I got back to class.

PARENT: What did she say to you? What did she say to Joseph?

CHILD: She just said that it will be OK and not to worry. She didn't say anything to Joseph.

With this additional information, you can develop a description of what happened in the cafeteria, what was said to your child, who heard it, whether your child told her teacher, and what the teacher did to stop it. The next step is to put a script together and contact the teacher—and then the principal, if you have to.

Script for Talking with a Middle School Child

PARENT: Who was sitting next to you on the bus when Tina punched you?

CHILD: Eddie was sitting there.

PARENT: Did the bus driver see what happened?

CHILD: No.

PARENT: Did anyone else see what Tina did to you?

CHILD: Yes. Frank and Nan saw, too.

Get the last names of the other kids, if any, who witnessed the bullying. Remember to record all of this information along with the day this happened.

PARENT: Did you tell anyone what Tina did to you?

CHILD: Yes. I told Mrs. Taylor when I got to class.

PARENT: What did she say to you? What did she say to Tina?

CHILD: She just said that it will be OK and not to worry. She didn't say anything to Tina.

With this additional information, you can develop a description of what happened on the bus, what was done to your child, who saw it, whether your child told her teacher, and what the teacher did to stop it. The next step is to put a script together and contact the teacher—and then the principal, if you have to.

Script for Talking with a High School Child

When you know that your high schooler is being bullied, this script can be useful for finding out more information.

> PARENT: Are those kids making you feel bad at school again?
>
> CHILD: Yes. They are telling stories about me, and now the other kids said I can't join the hockey team.
>
> PARENT: What stories are they telling about you?
>
> CHILD: They've been spreading rumors that I hooked up with John, and you know that's not true.
>
> PARENT: Exactly what are they saying?
>
> CHILD: They're saying that John and I are having sex. They say that no one who has sex can be on the hockey team.
>
> PARENT: Who are these kids?
>
> CHILD: Sam and Monica.
>
> PARENT: What are their last names?
>
> CHILD: Sam Irwin and Monica Elliott.
>
> PARENT: Did anyone else hear them say this?
>
> CHILD: Yes. Some of the kids in the cafeteria heard them: Phil, Jane, and Max.
>
> PARENT: What are their last names?
>
> CHILD: Phil Heywood, Jane Smith, and Max Walton.
>
> PARENT: Is there a teacher in the cafeteria? Is there a cafeteria monitor?

CHILD: Yes. Mrs. Martine.

PARENT: Did Mrs. Martine hear these kids say those things to you?

CHILD: Yes, she heard because she was standing right next to the table.

PARENT: What did she say to them?

CHILD: She told them that they are not allowed to talk like that and that it's against the school policy about bullying.

With this information, you have enough to develop a description of what happened, what was said, who said it, the names of those who were there to hear it, and what Mrs. Martine said. Now you can develop a script and call the principal to discuss what happened and to find out if Mrs. Martine ever reported Sam and Monica or whether she followed up on the school's policy.

Remember to use what you learned in chapter four about communicating effectively with the principal. Ask for a copy of the school's antibullying policy and document everything. Send a thank-you note recapping what you reported about the bullying and what the principal reported she did.

COMMON MISTAKES WHEN COMMUNICATING WITH YOUR CHILD

Here are some questions and comments that will shut down communication with your child or cause even more problems with the bully:

- How was your day (or how was school or how was the dance last night)?
- Why don't you just tell that bully to leave you alone?
- Why don't you just forget about it and let it go?

COMMUNICATING WITH THE SCHOOL AND
THE SCHOOL DISTRICT (CHAPTERS FOUR AND FIVE)

This section includes sample scripts and letters for communicating with teachers, principals, and superintendents. The level of accountability in public schools differs from that in private schools, so this section also includes examples for communicating with private school administrators.

HOW TO GET INFORMATION ABOUT YOUR CHILD'S SCHOOL DISTRICT

The first place to look for information about your child's school district is on the Internet. Enter the name of your school district and location, and search for its website. On that site, you will find the names of teachers, administrators, members of the board of education, and programs. It will also list contact information for the superintendent's office and the offices of principals and other administrators. It will not include phone numbers of members of the board of education; as you learned in chapter five, members cannot individually act as representatives of the board. Board members don't want parents or others in the community calling them with their personal gripes.

Teachers' email addresses and/or phone numbers are usually listed on the individual school's website. The school's site should also have a section that covers its protocol for addressing a complaint, how to get listed on the board of education's agenda to present a complaint, and whom to address when putting specific issues in writing.

TALKING WITH TEACHERS AND PRINCIPALS

In chapter four, we covered talking with your child's teacher before contacting the principal. Talking with the teacher is always a good place to start. Teachers participate in training on a regular basis. This training includes information about the school's antibullying policy and how it is to be implemented by teachers. But remember—if your child is still bullied after you contact the teacher, you will need to take it up a notch and go to the principal.

Script for Talking with Your Child's Teacher

PARENT: Hello, Mr. Kauffman. This is Madison Lubick's mother.

TEACHER: Hello, Ms. Lubick. Madison is a very nice girl, and she is a delight to have in class.

PARENT: Thank you. And I really appreciate your taking time out of your busy day to talk with me. I'm calling because I was reading the school's playground policy, and I have some questions about it.

TEACHER: Okay. How can I help you?

PARENT: How many kids are on the playground when Madison's class is there? And how many teachers are outside with them?

TEACHER: I think there are about two hundred students on the playground and two teacher assistants.

PARENT: Is it possible for two teacher assistants to watch all of the kids at the same time?

TEACHER: It's not easy, but I know the assistants. They're very careful.

PARENT: Well, Madison was pushed by two kids from another class, and she fell and cut her leg. This has happened before. I think she's being bullied.

TEACHER: Oh, I'm sorry. I know that she saw the nurse about the cut on her leg. Did she tell you who pushed her?

PARENT: Ray and John, from Ms. Finegold's class. What can you and I do together to help the situation so that Madison isn't pushed and hurt by them again?

Script for Talking with Your Child's Principal

A similar script for talking with the principal about the situation just described can be found in chapter four. There may be times when the quickest route to action is to place the responsibility squarely where it belongs—on the school administration. If your daughter was severely beaten in gym or if your son's arm was broken after being threatened by a group of other kids, you need to call the principal first. The script in chapter four is for a conversation with a public school principal. Here's a script for a phone call with a private school principal or headmaster.

> PARENT: Good morning, Dr. Thompson. This is Mr. Martin. Joey is my son. He's in fourth grade.
>
> PRINCIPAL: Good morning. I know Joey. He's a great kid. Isn't he in Mr. Johnson's class?
>
> PARENT: Yes, he is. The reason I'm calling this morning is that he's been harassed in class and on the playground by a couple of kids.
>
> PRINCIPAL: We have a very strict antiharassment policy at our school. In fact, we just had a workshop with teachers last week on this. Who are the kids who harassed Joey?
>
> PARENT: Sam and Wendy.
>
> PRINCIPAL: What are they doing?
>
> PARENT: They are calling Joey names and pushing him on the playground.
>
> PRINCIPAL: I'll talk with them about this and tell Mr. Johnson to watch what's happening.
>
> PARENT: What are the consequences for bullying and harassment in the school?
>
> PRINCIPAL: If Sam and Wendy continue to bully Joey after I talk with them, they'll receive a detention and I'll call their parents in for a conference.
>
> PARENT: Okay. Thanks for listening. I appreciate it very much.

COMMON MISTAKES WHEN COMMUNICATING
WITH TEACHERS AND PRINCIPALS

In chapter four, you learned how the right words, questions, and attitude will help you gain cooperation. Remember that the point isn't to put the teacher or principal on the spot but to build a respectful and reciprocal partnership to get your concerns resolved.

Communication is like electricity; when something works right, electricity flows from one source into another, and back to the first. Some words are confrontational and will short-circuit effective communication: *this instant* or *right now, I want you to, he/she better,* and *you have a problem in your school.* Similarly, phrasing questions a certain way can lead to defensive communication. Such questions often begin with *why didn't you* or *when are you going to.* In the conversation between Madison's mother and her teacher, notice how Ms. Lubick asked, "Is it possible for two teacher assistants to watch all of the kids at the same time?" If she had asked, "*How* is it possible for two teacher assistants to watch all of the kids at the same time?" she would have put the teacher on the defensive and short-circuited the direction of the discussion. Some other tips include the following:

- Avoid "you" remarks that criticize the person you are talking with instead of the action taken.
- Don't pretend to know more than the principal or teacher or pull rank with phrases like *you're new here.*
- Be informed before you speak if you claim to know what someone's responsibilities are (avoid the phrase *your job is to*). Even if you know that a school's antibullying policy compels the principal to take certain steps, calling him back to complain that he didn't won't be nearly as effective as putting it in a letter to his boss, the superintendent.

FOLLOW-UP LETTER TO THE PRINCIPAL OR HEADMASTER

After talking with the principal or headmaster, send him a thank-you letter and send a copy to the school district superintendent or the private school director. Reiterate the main points from your discussion and his commitment to resolve the issue. Here is a sample letter:

> Dr. Gerald Thompson, Headmaster
> Dear Dr. Thompson:
> Thank you for taking time out of your busy day to speak with me about Joey. I reported to you that Sam and Wendy were harassing Joey by calling him names and pushing him down on the playground.
>
> You told me that their behavior is against the school's rules and that you will talk to them about this. You also said that you would tell Mr. Johnson to watch out for this. Also, you said that if Sam and Wendy do this again that you will call their parents for a conference and they will receive a detention.
>
> I appreciate your follow-up and the seriousness with which you are taking this issue. Our school should always be welcoming and friendly—and bully free. Thanks for your help.
> Sincerely,
> James Martin

FOLLOW-UP LETTER TO THE SUPERINTENDENT

After you have a conversation with the principal and send a thank-you letter, give the process two weeks to simmer. Check in with your child to learn what's happening. If there are still problems, it's time to go up the ladder to the superintendent of the public school district or, in the case of a private school, the director or president.

Sample Letter to the Public School Superintendent

Donald Kennedy, Superintendent

Dear Dr. Kennedy:

I want to compliment you on your school's strong antibullying policy. I spoke with Mr. Williams recently about the policy and a problem that my daughter was having with two students. According to Mr. Williams, these students were violating the school's policy. He indicated to me that he would speak with the students and their parents, and that if the bullying occurred again, they would be disciplined. I appreciate all of his attention to this problem, because my daughter was negatively affected by this bullying.

That being said, however, I am afraid that the bullying is still continuing, even though I am sure Mr. Williams followed through.

At this time, I am seeking your intervention to ensure that the district's policy is followed. I would appreciate it if you would check with Mr. Williams to see what was actually done to stop the bullying, because it is still occurring.

If you would please check into this and give me a call at 555–0127 when you have a chance, I would greatly appreciate it.

Sincerely,

Jessica Lubick

copy: Mr. Williams

COMMUNICATING WITH BOARDS OF EDUCATION (CHAPTER FIVE)

When you send a letter requesting that the board of education address your concern, you are documenting that your child is being bullied; that the school has an antibullying policy; that you notified the principal and superintendent that she is being bullied in violation of the policy; that your child is still being bullied; that your child is being damaged as a result of the continued bullying; and that though the principal said she would do certain things, the bullying is continuing. Now, if you need to go further with a lawsuit, you have documentation. The response letter that you receive will also be an important document to keep for your records—especially if the bullying continues.

SAMPLE LETTER TO THE BOARD OF EDUCATION

Dr. Kenneth Stern, President

Dear Dr. Stern:

My daughter, Stephanie, is in Mr. Miller's sixth-grade class at Barley Sheaf School.

I talked with Ms. Adams, the principal, approximately four weeks ago about the school's antibullying policy. During our conversation, I let Ms. Adams know that three students from other classes have been harassing and bullying Stephanie in the cafeteria and on the playground during recess.

Ms. Adams explained the antibullying policy to me, and she said that she would speak with the students, their teachers, and their parents about what they have been doing to Stephanie. She also said that the students would receive in-school detention.

Two weeks later, I discussed this matter with Superintendent Schmidt, who said that he would follow up with Ms. Adams to find out what actions had been taken. Yet I am sorry to report that, after four weeks, Stephanie is still being bullied by these students. In fact, the bullying has intensified to the point where she is now coming home crying. Stephanie has also been experiencing nightmares and now doesn't want to go to school. Additionally, we are noticing a drop in her grades.

I am requesting a position on the board of education's meeting agenda to discuss my concerns about bullying. I am concerned not only about my daughter but also about whether the antibullying policy and student code of conduct are being followed.

Please feel free to call me at 555–0156 if you have any questions. Thank you in advance for your consideration.

Very truly yours,

Mary Pagan

Copy: Ms. Adams, Mr. Schmidt

SAMPLE LETTER TO THE PRIVATE SCHOOL BOARD OF DIRECTORS

Mrs. Jane Flanagan, President

Dear Mrs. Flanagan:

My son, James, is a student in Mr. Foster's ninth-grade class.

I know that you are interested in maintaining a peaceful and positive atmosphere at the school and that the staff is dedicated and hardworking. I also know that you and the board are interested in hearing from parents when there are any concerns.

I had a discussion with Mr. Manero, the headmaster, a couple of weeks ago about the fact that James is being hit and bullied by several students in Mr. Foster's class and other classes. This is happening, as I told Mr. Manero, in the locker room and gym class. Mr. Manero said that he would talk with the students and the gym teacher and that this would stop. However, it's still going on, and it has gotten worse. Yesterday, James came home with a black eye that he said he got from Fran in gym class.

I also talked with Dr. Miller, your school's director, who also said that this would stop. It is still going on.

I am now asking if you would please follow up with Dr. Miller to see why the bullying is still occurring and to have it stopped.

I would appreciate receiving a letter from you after you have
had a chance to follow up on this.

Truly yours,

Christina Farber

Copy: Dr. Miller

Because private schools are not subject to state antibullying laws,
you will not find the protection and force of the law when your
child is bullied in a private school. Private schools are in the business to make money to pay staff and administrators. Unfortunately,
in some circumstances, the school can make the decision not to accept your child for the next term—and you might not be able to do
anything about it. If this does happen, seek the advice of an attorney who is familiar with contracts—especially contracts between
parents and private schools.

COMMUNICATING WITH STATE AND FEDERAL GOVERNMENTS (CHAPTER FIVE)

STATE DEPARTMENTS OF EDUCATION

To find information about your state's department of education,
type your state's name and "Department of Education" into your
Internet browser. At your state's department of education website,
you will find information about safe and drug-free schools, bullying policy requirements, student performance in all districts across
the state, and how to file for a compliance investigation, as well as
additional useful information. The website should also include information about how to communicate with individuals in charge of
certain aspects of public and private school education. For example,
if your child with a disability is being bullied and her individualized
education program does not address strategies for her to deal with

bullying, you can contact the office of special education in your state's department of education to learn how that can be addressed.

Sample Letter of Complaint to Your State's Department of Education

Mr. Eugene Goldman, Director

Office of Special Education

Dear Mr. Goldman:

This is a letter of complaint against the Point Breeze Board of Education.

My son, Jonathan, is a senior at Point High School and is a child with a disability. Specifically, he suffers from neurological impairment that is manifested in obsessive-compulsive behavior and attention-deficit/hyperactivity disorder. Jonathan's individualized education plan specifically requires the district to provide a one-on-one classroom aide who will be with him during all his classes to coach him on academic and social-skills issues. The goal, according to the IEP, is for Jonathan to attend to academic requirements in the classroom and to be able to interact effectively with his peers.

For the past six months, the Point Breeze Board of Education has not provided the required aide. As a result, Jonathan has lost ground and is now being bullied by others in his class. He is not able to respond appropriately to these students due to his disability and his lack of social-skills development.

I have written numerous letters to the superintendent and board of education, copies of which are attached, but no one at the district level or at the level of the board of education has responded. Therefore, I am seeking the intervention of the State Department of Education in the form of this complaint.

Very truly yours,

Mrs. Michele Johnston

Each state's department of education must have a system for filing complaints. Complaints can be filed for various reasons, such as noncompliance with special-education regulations or a local board of education's nonresponsiveness, to name two. The website for your state's department of education will provide you with the information and steps to follow to have your voice heard.

Once the department of education receives your complaint, it will assess it to be sure that it complies with an issue that it can actually investigate. Next, you will receive a letter acknowledging that the department received your complaint and explaining what it plans to do about it. If the state decides to conduct an investigation, you will be provided with the results of the investigation and any directives provided to the school district as a result. You should hear from the state within two to four weeks.

FEDERAL OFFICE FOR CIVIL RIGHTS

The website of the Office for Civil Rights is located at http://www2 .ed.gov/about/offices/list/ocr/index.html. At this site, you can read an informative section entitled "Know Your Rights." If you believe that your child's school has violated her right to an education, then you can review another section entitled "How to File a Complaint." There, you will be escorted through the process of filing a complaint and submitting it over the Internet.

The U.S. Department of Education's Office for Civil Rights will determine whether it has jurisdiction over the issue stated in your complaint. You will receive a response indicating whether it will investigate and, if so, when you should receive a report. One thing to remember is that these complaints are filed in anonymity. The school is not informed of who files a complaint. Realistically, however, the issue behind the complaint most frequently identifies the complainant. You should know that you and your child are pro-tected from retaliation for filing a complaint, though you might need to keep an eye on how your child is treated once a complaint is filed.

COMMUNICATING WITH AN ATTORNEY (CHAPTER SIX)

The first place to search for an education-law attorney is your state's bar association. The American Bar Association website has a func-tion to help you find state and local bar associations; to find one, visit http://www.abanet.org/barserv/stlobar.html. Each state bar as-sociation's website should have a section listing lawyer specialties. Many state bar associations have education-law sections with a list of member attorneys who specialize in education law.

In addition to your state's bar association, you can search Mar-tindale (http://www.martindale.com), where lawyers pay to be listed. You can also search for education lawyers using standard search engines, such as Yahoo! or Google.

When you locate several choices in your state, carefully read each lawyer's profile and experience; many lawyers who list them-selves as "education lawyers" specialize in personal injury and may have had one or two education-related personal injury cases. Make a list. Before you call anyone, put your story together in very clear, concise terms. Lawyers typically don't have much time to talk with complaining parents on the phone.

When you call, ask to speak with a person who can tell you about the attorney's experience litigating school cases. You will likely be transferred to the attorney's paralegal if it's a medium- to large-sized office. If it's a small or single-person office, you will talk with the attorney herself. Have your story ready, and be brief.

Here's an example of what you might say:

PARENT: Good afternoon, Ms. Stockton. My name is Fran Pedderman. My daughter, Justine, goes to Franklin Township Middle School, and she's in the sixth grade.

ATTORNEY: Yes, Ms. Pedderman. How can I help you today?

PARENT: Franklin Township has an antibullying policy and a student code of conduct that addresses school bullying. My daughter has been called hurtful names like retarded, queer, gay, and other names. Also, out on the playground, she was pushed and fell. She had to go to the nurse. I talked with her teacher, who said that she would take care of it. Well, it went on for two more weeks and only got worse. Then I called the principal and told him what was happening. He said that he would investigate, discipline the students if necessary, and ask the teachers at a staff meeting to keep an eye out for Justine. I waited for a week or so and nothing happened. Finally, Justine was pushed so severely that she was knocked into a wall and broke her wrist. Her grades have gone from As and Bs to Ds, and she doesn't want to go to school anymore. Is there something that you can do to help?

ATTORNEY: Yes, I think I can help. Why don't you put everything in writing, make an appointment with my assistant, and come in to my office with Justine to talk this over. Bring a copy of the school policy and your daughter's student handbook so that we can go over it together. We'll figure out a way to address this.

PARENT: Thank you. I'll do that.

MORE ON DEALING WITH CYBERBULLYING
(CHAPTER SEVEN)

The U.S. Department of Health and Human Services offers these tips for dealing with a cyberbully:[1]

- Support your child; listen and empathize.
- Don't respond to the bully.
- Save the messages and images—don't erase them in case you need them for evidence.
- Report offensive language or other violations of the terms and conditions to email services and websites like Facebook, Yahoo!, and MySpace.
- Ask your Internet service provider to identify the cyberbully; the police may be able to help if you think the harassment crosses criminal lines.
- Block the cyberbully's email or cell phone harassment if you are able; contact your Internet or cell phone service providers to see if this is possible.
- Remember from chapter seven that your school is obligated to intervene if the harassment comes through the school district's Internet system. Administrators should also be made aware of the situation if it occurs outside of the school.
- Consider telling the bully's parents if you think that they might help; as you would do with the school, documenting the episode in writing can be useful, especially if you can show printouts or other evidence of cyberbullying.
- Consider contacting an attorney; in serious cases, victims may be able to sue the cyberbully.
- Contact the police if you think the actions are criminal; if you aren't sure, your local police should be able to advise you.

HOW TO SET UP SECURITY SETTINGS TO STOP AN ONLINE BULLY

You can protect your child by fighting back online—not by responding to bullying messages, but by using tools that can help you find and remove hurtful content. Note that these methods were accurate and effective at the time this book was published. In the fast-changing cyberworld, things may have already improved to help you protect your child. My suggestion is to do some research on the site where the offense occurs to see what new ways are offered to protect your child. The most popular email and social networking sites, such as Yahoo!, Hotmail, Google, Facebook, and MySpace, are prepared to handle trouble. These sites allow you to remove comments, delete friends, and report abuse. You can also restrict what others see and can say about your child by using the site's privacy settings.

Social Networking Sites

On Facebook, you can report a bully or take him off of your child's friend list by going to your child's profile and clicking "Report/Block This Person" or "Remove from Friends." You also can report malicious content on group pages by clicking "Report Page" and identifying the offensive content. People in photos can dissociate themselves from hateful content by clicking on the photo and selecting "Remove Tag" beside their name. If nudity or other Facebook violations are involved, report it to Facebook, which may take the offending item down.

On MySpace, you can block an abuser from your child's profile page and report him by clicking "Contact MySpace" at the bottom of any page. MySpace also offers a preference that allows people to preapprove all comments made on their profiles; under "Settings," select "Spam" and choose "Require Approval Before Comments Are Posted."

If your child finds a mean comment or question on Formspring—a relatively new social networking site—know that if she doesn't answer it, nobody will see it. You can also block the author from contacting your child again. To report bullies, click "Help" on any page and file a complaint. You can adjust privacy settings to block anonymous questions and to approve the people who can "follow" your child.

Email Providers

Major web-based email services also have codes of conduct that prohibit harassment, and have tools that you can use to report bad behavior.

In Hotmail, choose "Options" at the top of any page, find the "Blocked Senders" button, and add the email addresses of those who are bullying your child. In Gmail, you can set up a filter that detects offending addresses and choose to automatically delete future messages sent from those addresses. There also is a setting that allows you to forward those messages to you or another adult. In Yahoo! Mail, choose "Help" at the top left of the page, select "Report Abuse," and follow the instructions.

Instant messages typically come from only those people whom a user has added to her chat list. Abusers are usually easy to block and report.

If your child's bullying is occurring by way of abusive phone calls and text messages, blocking them requires visiting your carrier's website, logging into your account, and adding in the problem phone numbers. It cannot be done from the cell phone. Some cell phone providers charge a monthly fee for this service.

Several online services and software programs can help you detect and address online bullying. You can install parent-control software on the computers that your children use; it comes in free and paid versions from several companies. Some, for instance, monitor social network usage and oversee certain chat lists and instant messaging conversations.

You also can monitor text messages on smartphones. Products exist that can scan for words and phrases that may be offensive.

SAVING THE EVIDENCE

In serious situations, such as when there are threats of violence, you will need evidence to show the police. Take screenshots or save copies of web pages and email messages, instant messages, and texts.

If your case is taken to court, it is best to have digital evidence obtained directly from online services and the bully's own computer. Keep in mind that the online services do not keep data forever and that bullies can wipe their hard drives clean if they know that they are being investigated. In this case, the easiest and best way to preserve evidence is to enlist law enforcement, which can confiscate a bully's computer and, with the help of a computer expert, can extract an electronic paper trail.

THE BULLY ACTION GUIDE INTERACTIVE WEBSITE

A special website has been set up for you to learn even more about bullying. On this site, www.thebullyactionguide.com, you will find the following:

- other websites on bullying
- other books and resources for further reading for parents, teachers, and administrators about the phenomena of bullying and cyberbullying
- important references on disability
- links to Title IX, Section 504, IDEA, and Title II
- legal resources (websites)
- statistical data and listings of studies on bullying behavior

Also, at this special website, you will be able to communicate with me at any time about your questions.

NOTES

INTRODUCTION

1. The last names of Patrick and his mother, Beth, have been changed here and throughout this book to protect their privacy.

CHAPTER ONE: THE MANY FACES OF BULLYING

Note: All quotations that do not indicate a source are from conversations between the author and the subject.

1. Olweus, D. (1993). *Bullying at School: What We Know and What We Can Do.* Cambridge, MA: Blackwell.
2. Nansel, T. R., Overpeck, M., Pilla, R. S., Ruan, W. J., Simons-Morton, B., and Scheidt, P. (April 25, 2001). "Bullying Behaviors among U.S. Youth: Prevalence and Association with Psychosocial Adjustment." *Journal of the American Medical Association* 286 (16), 2094–2100.
3. Nansel and others (April 25, 2001).
4. Wang, J., Iannotti, R. J., Nansel, T. R. (October 2009). "School Bullying among U.S. Adolescents: Physical, Verbal, Relational, and Cyber." *Journal of Adolescent Health* 45 (4), 368–375.
5. Kowalski, R. M., Limber, S. P., and Agatston, P. W. (2008). *Cyberbullying: Bullying in the Digital Age.* Malden, MA: Blackwell.
6. Batsche, G. M., and Knoff, H. M. (1994). "Bullies and Their Victims: Understanding a Pervasive Problem in the Schools." *School Psychology Review* 23 (2), 165–174.
7. Vossekuil, B., Reddy, M., Fein R., Borum, R., and Modzeleski, W. (October 2000). *Safe School Initiative: An Interim Report on the Prevention of Targeted Violence in Schools.* Washington, DC: U.S. Secret Service, National Threat Assessment Center, 7.
8. Batsche and Knoff (1994), 165–174.
9. McWilliams, M. (March 14, 2010). "'Loser' Remark Directed at Student by Enka Middle School Teacher Probed." *Asheville Citizen-Times.* http://www.citizen-times.com/article/20100314/NEWS/303140069/

-Loser-remark-directed-at-student-by-Enka-Middle-School-teacher-probed.

10. Kolodner, M. (February 23, 2010). "Mom Claims Kindergarten Bullies at Brooklyn's PS 161 Punched Daughter, 5, and Cut off Her Hair." *New York Daily News.* http://www.nydailynews.com/ny_local/education/2010/02/23/2010-02-23_look_what_school_bullies_did_to_me.html.

11. Ahmad, Y., and Smith, P. K. (1994). "Bullying in Schools and the Issues of Sex Difference." In J. Archer, *Male Violence.* London: Routledge, 70–83.

12. Olweus (1993).

13. Olweus (1993).

14. Oliver, R., Hoover, J. H., and Hazler, R. (1994). "The Perceived Roles of Bullying in Small-Town Midwestern Schools." *Journal of Counseling and Development* 72 (4), 416–419.

15. Olweus (1993).

16. Nansel and others (April 25, 2001).

17. Hoover, J. H., and Oliver, R. (1996). *The Bullying Prevention Handbook: A Guide for Principals, Teachers, and Counselors.* Bloomington, IN: National Education Service, 5–16.

18. Nansel (2001).

19. Currie, C., Samdal, O., Boyce, W., and Smith, B. (2001). Health Behaviour in School-Aged Children: A World Health Organization Cross-National Study. Research Protocol for the 2001/02 Survey. Child and Adolescent Health Research Unit, University of Edinburgh: Edinburgh, Scotland.

20. Wang (2009).

21. Charach, A., Pepler, D., and Ziegler, S. (1995). "Bullying at School—a Canadian Perspective: A Survey of Problems and Suggestions for Intervention." *Education Canada* 35 (1), 12–18.

22. Olweus, D., Limber, S., and Mihalic, S. (1999). *Blueprints for Violence Prevention, Book Nine: Bullying Prevention Program.* Boulder, CO: Center for the Study and Prevention of Violence.

23. Arsenault, L., Walsh, E., Trzesniewski, K., Newcombe R., Caspi, A., and Moffitt, T. E. (2006). "Bullying Victimization Uniquely Contributes to Adjustment Problems in Young Children: A Nationally Representative Cohort Study." *Pediatrics* 118 (1), 130–138.

24. *Boston Herald* staff. (April 9, 2010). "Court Papers: Phoebe Prince's Life 'Intolerable.'" *Boston Herald.*

25. Cathcart, R. (February 23, 2008). "Boy's Killing, Labeled a Hate Crime, Stuns a Town." *New York Times.* http://www.nytimes.com/2008/02/23/us/23oxnard.html?_r=1&pagewanted=print.

26. In this chapter, the names of Stephanie, Janet, and Daryl have been changed.

27. Associated Press (November 30, 2009). "3 Boys Detained for California 'Ginger Day' Attacks." http://www.chron.com/disp/story.mpl/nation/6746451.html.

CHAPTER TWO: WHY YOU CAN'T COUNT ON SCHOOLS

1. Farrington, D. (1993). "Understanding and Preventing Bullying." In M. Tonry (ed.), *Crime and Justice: A Review of Research,* vol.17. Chicago and London: University of Chicago Press.

2. Hoover, J., Oliver, R., and Haxler, R. (1992). "Bullying: Perceptions of Adolescent Victims in the Midwestern USA." *School Psychology International* 13 (1), 5–16.

3. Salmivalli, C. (1999). "Participant Role Approach to School Bullying Implications for Intervention." *Journal of Adolescence* 22 (4), 453–459. See also Olweus, D., and Limber, S. (1999). "Bullying Prevention Program." In D. Elliott (ed.), *Blueprints for Violence Prevention.* Boulder, CO: Institute of Behavioral Science, Regents of the University of Colorado.

4. South Hadley High School District Policies Subgroup. (February 23, 2010). Meeting minutes, 2.

5. South Hadley High School District Policies Subgroup. (March 1, 2010). Meeting minutes, 3.

6. U.S. Department of Education Office for Civil Rights (January 1999). Protecting Students from Harassment and Hate Crime: A Guide for Schools. Part II: Step-by-Step Guidance. http://www2.ed.gov/offices/OCR/archives/Harassment/policy1.html.

7. Gittlin, R., and Dahle, S. (June 14, 2008). "Teen's Family Sues Middle School after Bullying." ABC News. http://abcnews.go.com/GMA/Week end/story?id=5126830&page=1.

8. Szaniszlo, M., and Crimaldi, L. (April 1, 2010). "DA Responds to South Hadley Superintendent." *Boston Herald.* http://www.bostonherald.com/news/regional/view.bg?articleid=1243994.

CHAPTER THREE: HOW TO GET THE FACTS: WHAT QUESTIONS TO ASK YOUR CHILD

1. In this chapter, as well as in chapters four and five, "Lisa" is one of my clients. I have changed her first name to protect her privacy.

2. Ruder, D. B. (September–October 2008). "The Teen Brain." *Harvard Magazine* 111 (1), 8.

3. Trotter, A. (January 12, 2005). "Brain Research Invoked to Explain Teens' Behavior." *Education Week* 24 (18), 8.

4. Blakemore, S-J. (September 7, 8, 2006). "The Social Brain: the Mirror System, Autism, and Adolescence." Presented at: British Association Festival of Science, Norwich, United Kingdom, September 8, 2006.

5. Goudarzi, S. (September 8, 2006). "Study: Teenage Brain Lacks Empathy." MSNBC.com. http://www.msnbc.msn.com/id/14738243/ns/technology _and_science-science.

6. Goudarzi (September 8, 2006).

CHAPTER FOUR: HOW TO APPROACH THE SCHOOL

1. Not her real name.

2. Not her real name.

CHAPTER FIVE: WHAT TO DO WHEN YOU GET NO RESULTS

1. Goldman, G., Lennon, D., and Dalton, D. (July 6, 2010). "School Officials Should Have Stopped Bullying." Letter to the editor. *Adirondack Daily Enterprise.* http://www.adirondackdailyenterprise.com/page/content .detail/id/514187/School-officials-should-have-stopped-bullying.html ?nav=5005.

2. Farrington, D. (1993). "Understanding and Preventing Bullying." In M. Tonry (ed.), *Crime and Justice: A Review of Research, Vol.* 17. Chicago and London: University of Chicago Press.

3. Goldman (July 6, 2010).

4. Eaton, W. E. (1990). *Shaping the Superintendency.* New York: Teachers College Press, Columbia University; Snowden, P. E., and Gorton, R. A. (1998). *School Leadership and Administration,* 5th ed. New York: Mc-Graw-Hill.

5. Campbell, D. W., and Green, D. (1994). "Defining the Leadership Role of School Boards in the 21st Century." *Phi Delta Kappan* 75 (5),391–395; Good, H. (1998). "Governance: Then and Now." *American School Board Journal* 185 (5), 50–51.

6. Sade, V. (May 7, 2009). "Distraught Parents Voice Bullying Concerns to School Board." *Busco Voice.* http://www.buscovoice.com/2009/05/07/distraught-parents-voice-bullying-concerns-to-school-board.

7. Saline Area Schools. (2010). "Meet the Board of Education and the Superintendent." http://www.salineschools.com/index.php/board-of-education.

8. Toledo Public Schools. (2010). "Making a Presentation to the Board." http://www.tps.org/Board_of_Education.

9. Section 504 is a part of the Rehabilitation Act of 1973. IDEA is the acronym for the Individuals with Disabilities Education Act. Title II is a section of the Americans with Disabilities Act.

10. Appropriate classroom discipline is permissible. This generally constitutes the type of discipline that is applied to all students or is consistent with the Individuals with Disabilities Education Act and Section 504, including each student's individualized education program or Section 504 plan.

11. Paige, R. (September 19, 2001). "Prohibited Racial or Ethnic Harassment— Reminder of Responsibilities under Title VI of the Civil Rights Act of 1964." Dear colleague letter.

12. Office for Civil Rights. (Oct. 20, 2010.) "How to File a Discrimination Complaint with the Office for Civil Rights." http://www2.ed.gov/about/offices/list/ocr/docs/howto.html?src=rt.

CHAPTER SIX: THE LEGAL FACE OF BULLYING: CRIMINAL AND CIVIL LAWS

1. Fuller, N. (April 13, 2010). "Parents of Slain Crofton Teen File $10 Million Lawsuit." *Baltimore Sun.* http://articles.baltimoresun.com/2010–04–

13/news/bs-ar-crofton-gang-lawsuit13–20100413_1_christopher-david-jones-crofton-youths.

2. Hayes, C. (August 2, 2010). "Jeremy Prince: School to Blame for Phoebe's Suicide Not Teens on Trial." *IrishCentral.com*. http://www.irishcentral.com/news/Jeremy-Prince-School-to-blame-for-Phoebes-suicide-not-teens-on-trial–99747624.html?page=2.

3. Bully Police USA (2010). "The Commonwealth of Massachusetts A++." http://www.bullypolice.org/ma_law.html.

4. WMUR.com (July 8, 2010). "New Law Gives Teachers Tools to Battle Bullies." http://www.wmur.com/print/24187070/detail.html.

5. Abramson, L. (March 25, 2010). "Hit Back at Bullies? Not at This School." National Public Radio. http://www.npr.org/templates/story/story.php?storyId=125137071.

6. Bentances, Y. (June 10, 2009). "Students Learn Ways to Stop Bullies." *Eagle-Tribune* (Lawrence, MA). http://www.eagletribune.com/local/x1650958884/Students-learn-ways-to-stop-bullies.

7. Kukla, M. (June 10, 2010.) "Anti-bullying Program in Saugatuck Schools Reports Surprising Success." *Grand Rapids Press*. http://www.mlive.com/a2z/index.ssf/2010/06/anti-bullying_program_in_saugatuck_schools_reports_surprising_success.html.

8. Chaker, A. M. (January 24, 2007). "Schools Move to Stop Spread of Cyberbullying." *Wall Street Journal*. http://online.wsj.com/article/SB116960763498685883.html (subscription required); also available at http://www.postgazette.com/pg/07024/756408–96.stm#ixzz0yqpmgtla.

9. Brunsman, B. J. (July 19, 2010). "Milford Bullying Suit Dismissed." *Cincinnati.com*. http://news.cincinnati.com/article/AB/20100719/NEWS010702/7200337/Milford-bullying-suit-dismissed.

10. Contrada, F. (July 27, 2010). "South Hadley Middle School Bullying Civil Case Settled out of Court." *The Republican*. http://www.masslive.com/news/index.ssf/2010/07/south_hadley_middle_school_bul.html.

11. Gomez, A. (May 14, 2010). "5 NH Students Charged in Bullying Probe." *WBZ-TV*. http://wbztv.com/local/bully.Salem.High.2.1694364.html.

12. Rubinkam, M. (May 28, 2010). "Autistic Kids Abused in Pennsylvania Classroom to Get $5M." *ABC News*. http://abcnews.go.com/US/wireStory?id=10770887.

13. Title IX of the Education Amendments of 1972.

14. Greenwald, J. (April 18, 2010). "Schools Work to Reduce Liabilities over Bullying." *Business Insurance*. http://www.businessinsurance.com/article/20100418/ISSUE01/304189972.

15. Bazelon, E. (July 29, 2010). "Talking to Phoebe Prince's Father." *Slate.com*. http://www.slate.com/toolbar.aspx?action=print&id=2262194.

16. Guilfoil, J. M. (August 10, 2010). "Defense Lawyers Seek Medical Records in Prince Case." *Boston Globe*. http://www.boston.com/news/education/k_12/articles/2010/08/10/defense_lawyers_seek_medical_records_in_prince_case/.

17. Broman, A. (August 4, 2010). "Chequamegon School District Sued over Alleged Failure to Stop Bullying." *Ashland Current.* http://ashland current.com/article/10/08/04/chequamegon-school-district-sued-over-alleged-failure-stop-bullying-updated; Murphy, K. (August 4, 2010). "Park Falls School District, Staff Sued over Alleged Student Bullying, Neglect." *The Daily Press.* http://www.ashlandwi.com/articles/2010/08/04/news/doc4c5a324fd79bc391264485.txt.

18. Mandak, J. (August 4, 2010). "Judge OKs $55K Anorexia Bullying Settlement in Pennsylvania." *Centredaily.com.* http://www.centredaily.com/2010/08/04/2131843/lawyer-cant-find-plaintiff-in.html; Ward, P. R. (August 4, 2010). "Pittsburgh Public Schools Settle Suit over Girl's Anorexia, Taunting. *Pittsburgh Post-Gazette.* http://www.post-gazette.com/pg/10216/1077392–53.stm#ixzz0wKVJmpUY.

19. Davis, as next friend of LaShonda D., v. Monroe County Board of Education et al. (Argued January 12, 1999; decided May 24, 1999). Certiorari to the United States Court of Appeals for the Eleventh Circuit, no. 97–843, 2.

20. Davis (1999), 12.

21. Davis (1999), 17.

22. United States Department of Labor (1972). "Title IX, Education Amendments of 1972 (Title 20 U.S.C. Sections 1681–1688)." http://www.dol.gov/oasam/regs/statutes/titleix.htm.

CHAPTER SEVEN: BULLYING ON THE CYBER PLAYGROUND

1. Bartlett, S. (August 6, 2010). "Parents Seek to End Cyber Bullying." *Press-Republican.* http://pressrepublican.com/new_today/x91132313/Parents-seek-end-to-cyber-bullying.

2. Bartlett (August 6, 2010).

3. Bartlett (August 6, 2010).

4. Bartlett (August 6, 2010).

5. Henry J. Kaiser Family Foundation. (2010). *Generation M2 Media in the Lives of 8- to 18-Year-Olds: A Kaiser Family Foundation Study.* http://www.kff.org/entmedia/mh012010pkg.cfm.

6. Henry J. Kaiser Family Foundation (2010).

7. Henry J. Kaiser Family Foundation (2010).

8. Chitlangia, R. (July 6, 2010). "Bullying Moves from Classroom into Cyberspace." *Times of India.* http://timesofindia.indiatimes.com/articleshow/6133020.cms.

9. Struglinski, S. (August 18, 2006). "Schoolyard Bullying Has Gone High-Tech." *Deseret Morning News.* http://www.deseretnews.com/article/645194065/Schoolyard-bullying-has-gone-high-tech.html.

10. Steinhauer, J. (November 21, 2008). "Woman Who Posed as Boy Testifies in Case that Ended in Suicide of 13-Year-Old." *New York Times.* http://www.nytimes.com/2008/11/21/us/21myspace.html.

11. Shaw, L. (January 15, 2010). "Cyberbullying Leads to Suspension of 28 Middle Schoolers at McClure." *Seattle Times.* http://seattletimes.nwsource.com/html/localnews/2010807798_mcclure16m.html.

12. Blanchard, J. (November 28, 2008). "Cheerleaders' Parents Sue in Nude Photos Incident." *Seattle Post-Intelligencer.* http://www.seattlepi.com/local/388940_bothell22.html.
13. iSafe. (2009). "Cyberbullying: Statistics and Tips." http://www.isafe.org/channels/sub.php?ch=op&sub_id=media_cyber_bullying.
14. Cox Communications. (2009). "Teen Online & Wireless Safety Survey: Cyberbullying, Sexting, and Parental Controls." http://www.cox.com/takecharge/safe_teens_2009/research.html.
15. Fight Crime: Invest in Kids. (2006). "Cyber Bully Pre-teen." www.fight-crime.org/cyberbullying/cyberbullyingpreteen.pdf.
16. Kowalski, R. N., and Limber, S. P. (2007). "Electronic Bullying among Middle School Students." *Journal of Adolescent Health* 41, S22–S30.
17. Hinduja, S., and Patchin, J. W. (2008). "Cyberbullying: An Exploratory Analysis of Factors Related to Offending and Victimization." *Deviant Behavior* 29,(2), 129–136.
18. Figures add up to more than 100 percent because a student could be cyberbullied by more than one person.
19. Kowalski, R. M., Limber, S. P., and Agatston, P. W. (2008). *Cyber Bullying: Bullying in the Digital Age.* Malden, MA: Blackwell.
20. Shoemaker-Galloway, J. (2007). "Cyberbullying Methods: The Various Tactics Used to Bully Online." *Suite101.com.* http://www.suite101.com/content/online-bullying-a22759.
21. Agatston, P. W., Kowalski, R., and Limber, S. (2007). "Students' Perspectives on Cyber Bullying." *Journal of Adolescent Health* 41, S59–S60.
22. Ginter, M. (August 16, 2010). "District Ponders Subjecting Students to Cell Phone Search." *KOMOnews.com.* http://www.komonews.com/news/local/100809309.html.
23. Cyberbully Alert (October 13, 2008). Stories of Cyber Bullying. http://www.cyberbullyalert.com/blog/page/2/.
24. Bully Police USA (2006). Idaho. http://www.bullypolice.org/id_law.html.
25. Bully Police USA (2007). Iowa. http://www.bullypolice.org/ia_law.html
26. National Conference of State Legislatures (2007). RS 14:40.2. http://www.legis.state.la.us/lss/lss.asp?doc=78515.
27. Cyberbully Alert (October 13, 2008).
28. Cyberbully Alert (October 13, 2008).
29. Bully Police USA (2010). New York. http://www.bullypolice.org/ny_law.html.
30. Cyberbully Alert (October 13, 2008).
31. Cyberbully Alert (October 13, 2008).
32. Steinhauer (November 21, 2008).
33. Chicago Public Schools (2010). "Student Resources: Student Code of Conduct." http://www.cps.edu/Pages/StudentResourcesStudentCodeofConduct.aspx.
34. eSchool News (July 29, 2010). "Chicago Public Schools Crack Down on Cyberbullies." http://www.eschoolnews.com/2010/07/29/chicago-public-schools-crack-down-on-cyber-bullies.

35. Center for Safe and Responsible Internet Use. (2010). "Cyberbullying: Mobilizing Educators, Parents, Students, and Others to Combat Online Social Cruelty." http://www.cyberbully.org/cyberbully/.
36. *Finkel v. Dauber.* (July 22, 2010). WL 2872874 (New York Supreme Court).

APPENDIX

1. Health Resources and Services Administration, U.S. Department of Health and Human Services (2010). "Stop Bullying Now!–Cyberbullying." http://www.stopbullyingnow.hrsa.gov/adults/cyber-bullying.aspx.

INDEX